Deepak Bajaj is an ace motivational speaker, India's leading success trainer, a high-performance coach and a #1 bestselling author of 2 books.

A master of personal transformation, Deepak has been on a mission to inspire and empower people to be the best they can be for the last 2 decades. Deepak is an expert in human behavior and success psychology who not only delivers insights, tools and strategies but also works deep on people's beliefs and emotions to bring instant change and lasting transformation. Millions of people from 100-plus countries have been achieving their dreams faster with his books, live events, online courses and video training.

Deepak's books, *Be a Network Marketing Millionaire* and *Achieve More, Succeed Faster*, have been established as the most read and recommended books in the direct selling industry. His books have been translated into 8 languages so far and are considered to be the definitive guidebooks for every direct seller.

Deepak's live events and online courses have been globally recognized for their incredible results, and more than 11 lakh people have already attended his training sessions. He has been featured in various magazines and has received various awards, like Best Direct Selling Trainer of 2020, Best Debut Author of 2018, Best Entrepreneurship Trainer and Coach etc. He is a regular keynote speaker at various events and is looked upon as the lighthouse of the direct selling industry. He is also a consultant to many leading companies, helping them multiply their sales and performance.

With his vast global experience spanning more than 18 years, Deepak Bajaj has become a brand unto himself, garnering iconic stature in the industry.

Follow him on all major social media platforms and at www.deepakbajaj.biz.

BE A SOCIAL MEDIA MILLIONAIRE

Tips and Techniques to Build your Brand and
Multiply your Direct Selling Business Online

DEEPAK BAJAJ

First published in India by

Manjul Publishing House
- C-16, Sector 3, Noida, Uttar Pradesh 201301, India
  Website: www.manjulindia.com
  Registered Office:
- 10, Nishat Colony, Bhopal 462 003 – India
  Distribution Centres:
  Ahmedabad, Bengaluru, Bhopal, Kolkata, Chennai, Hyderabad, Mumbai, New Delhi, Pune

Copyright © by Deepak Bajaj, 2021
All rights reserved.

This edition first published in 2021
Third impression 2021

ISBN 978-93-5543-015-1

Cover design © PealiDezine, peali.duttagupta@gmail.com

Printed and bound in India by Nutech Print Services-India

This publication is designed to provide competent and reliable information regarding the subject matter covered. However, it is sold with the understanding that the author and publisher are not engaged in rendering legal, financial, or other professional advice. If legal or other expert assistance is required, the services of a professional should be sought. The author and publisher specifically disclaim any liability that is incurred from the use or application of the contents of this book.

All rights reserved. No part of this publication may be reproduced, stored in or introduced into a retrieval system, or transmitted, in any form, or by any means (electronic, mechanical, photocopying, recording or otherwise) without the prior written permission of the publisher. Any person who does any unauthorized act in relation to this publication may be liable to criminal prosecution and civil claims for damages.

Dedication

THIS BOOK IS DEDICATED to each and every one of you who not only have dreams but also have the drive and commitment to work for those dreams.

I want to support you on your journey to achieve your dreams through this book. This book is a toolkit of inspiration, insights, techniques and solutions that you can instantly apply to fast-forward your way to success.

The rules of success have totally changed in the last couple of years. COVID-19 has further accelerated the speed of change and has taught us many invaluable lessons. This book is a total personal and business transformation tool that will empower you to achieve massive success using social media in this new, changed world.

Growing up in a village, studying in local schools, facing financial struggles, moving from a job to entrepreneurship, making mistakes and starting all over again from zero ... I have been through all of it and I know how it feels. Trust me, every legend started from zero and has endured hardship and rejection. I know you have the seeds of greatness inside you and this book is my attempt to bring out the legend in you.

Now is your time to rise.

Go for your dreams.

Stay unstoppable.

Feedback for Deepak's Books and Courses

"Deepak Bajaj is India's leading direct selling expert. His work is showing people the way to change life."
— **Sh. Som Parkash, Union Minister for Industries and Commerce, Govt. of India**

"Every direct seller and those who target to become a millionaire should read this book."
— **Kailash Bhattad, CEO, Mi Lifestyle Marketing Global Private Limited**

"Backed by 13 years' experience and over 8 lakh followers and trainees, Deepak has been working untiringly for the upliftment of direct sellers with his bestselling books, online courses, training programs and free videos."
— **Direct Selling Today magazine**

"Deepak Bajaj is India's #1 Authority on Network Marketing, an Entrepreneurship consultant, a Life Coach, a Transformational Trainer and an Inspirational Speaker all rolled into one."
— **Invincible Magazine**

"One of the best books on how to achieve big in network marketing. It's a perfect gift for the teammates to make them serious in business."
— **Mubeen Muhammad**

"Deepak's books are like the Geeta or Quran of network marketing."
— **Dr. Akhtar Khanwala**

"Deepak Sir's courses are a million-dollar jackpot at a throwaway price. These are the best programs anyone can get."
— **Suveer Singh**

"Every time I open my social media accounts, they are full of notifications. I have started getting so many leads and prospects that I sometime wonder how to handle all of them. I have got much more than I expected from Deepak Bajaj's Social Media and Online Business Mastery course."
— **Sachidanand Tripathi**

"The best part about Deepak Bajaj's training is duplication. My entire team is able to follow his concepts easily."
— **Rashmi Saxena**

"All the mindset, skillsets and toolsets that you need for building a big business has been covered in one single course — Ultimate Network Marketing Mastery."
— **Shuchi Caire**

"What I could not learn in 20 years of my network marketing career I have got through Deepak Bajaj's Ultimate Network Marketing Course. It's out of the world."
— **Jay Prakash Maurya**

"Deepak Bajaj's courses are not just about building business but also about how to live life in the right way. It has totally changed every aspect of my life."
— **Kiran John**

"This one book is enough for success in direct selling."

— **Mukesh Singh**

"I have become unstoppable. I got 10 years ahead with this great book."

— **Lomesh Choudhary**

"This book will help all those people who really want to do something in life."

— **Mahendra Singh Rawat**

"My fear of social media has disappeared and my business is growing like crazy after doing the social media course by Deepak Bajaj. Every promise that was given about the course has been delivered to the fullest."

— **Supriya Kothadia**

"I have become a totally different person after attending Deepak Sir's course. Everyone around me is giving me compliments, saying that I have changed a lot, and my business is also growing."

— **Nargis Sultana**

"I got the answers to all my questions. It has made my business skyrocket."

— **Nitu Jindal**

"This is the book which can change the lives of all and can fulfill the dreams of people who dream of becoming rich."

— **Harshada Nikam**

"After doing Deepak Sir's course, I am feeling such positive vibes which I have never felt before. The Ultimate Network Marketing Mastery course is not just for business results; it's a life transformation course that will help you everywhere in life."

— **Viren Jumani**

"I am confidently making and posting videos on social media. I am getting leads and actually creating my prospecting pool."

— **Janhvi Singh**

"The most amazing book I have ever read in my life. This book changed my thinking. I have become a totally different person after reading this book. I will be a millionaire."

— **Alka P.**

"This book is the Bible, Bhagavad Gita and Quran of network marketing. Need no other book to follow after reading this book."

— **Arun Singh**

"Excellent book. Highly recommended. Such appropriate and structured content in every page of this book."

— **Gaurav Mehra**

"One-stop solution for network marketing. Strongly recommended for those who want to avoid mistakes and achieve success faster."

— **Vijay Tetarwal**

"Amazing books for beginners, doers, experts and trainers."

— **Pradeep Choudhery**

Deepak Bajaj's Direct Selling Journey

THE TRANSFORMATION OF DEEPAK Bajaj from a shy village boy to one of the top performers and then to a leading direct selling trainer and consultant is a source of inspiration and strength for everyone. Deepak has come a long way and is living proof of what can be achieved with clear vision, absolute faith, the right values and absolute commitment.

Deepak was born into a family of government employees in a very small village in Haryana, India and studied in different Hindi medium government schools. His father passed away after a two-year-long battle with cancer when Deepak was 8 years old. Deepak had a tough childhood laden with financial challenges, adjustments and compromises. But all these years, Deepak grew up with one dream – *"One day, I will be a big man."*

Determined to make it big, Deepak cleared the CAT exam and completed his MBA from a leading management institute. He started his corporate career with a sales job in a leading automobile MNC and rose quickly to the rank of regional manager in record time. This was the time when someone approached him to join their direct selling business, in May 2006. For the next 13 months, different people approached him regarding their direct selling business, but he was not convinced.

On 28 June 2007, he decided to start his direct selling business and work on it part-time alongside his job. He started working aggressively with a game plan, which is now famous across the world as the 90-day game plan. He worked day and night non-stop for the next 3 months on a grueling schedule, created new records in direct selling and resigned his corporate job within 3 months, on 30 Sep 2007. Deepak was excellent at sales but he had no experience with direct selling. He did not have any training programs, his teammates could not duplicate his working style and his business came crashing to the ground, putting his family through their worst financial crisis ever for the next nine months. It was a tough phase and all his relatives and friends suggested he go back to his job. Any ordinary person would have quit in that situation and even Deepak felt like quitting a few times. But instead, he worked harder, learned more and continued moving forward with the philosophy that what doesn't break you, makes you stronger.

He became a student of the business and started learning the best success practices across the globe. The more rejections he faced, the more time and money he invested into his training and development. He then started creating programs and systems that were never heard of before in the industry and set record after record in the business. As he started expanding his business in multiple locations, he faced many challenges along the way; many of his teams crashed, but every failure became a learning experience and Deepak used each one to improve his system. He also created duplicable tools that anyone could use anywhere to grow their business, irrespective of their age, background, location, education, gender or financial status. Those systems and tools turned his business into a passive income generating machine from January 2009 onwards.

Lakhs of people in several different network marketing companies have already fulfilled their dreams and achieved top ranks in their companies using his tools and systems. His two books, *Be a Network Marketing Millionaire* and *Achieve More, Succeed Faster* are the most read and recommended books in the entire direct selling industry. These books have been translated into 8 languages and direct sellers in every company are advised to read these books before they enter the business. These books are full of strategies, tools, techniques and insights that can help anyone to achieve massive success in the business as well as in life.

With close to fifteen years of incredible experience, Deepak has become a brand unto himself and is considered a living legend in the direct selling industry. He has been awarded the title of Best Direct Selling Trainer of 2020. He has been featured in various magazines and has received various awards like Best Debut Author of 2018, Best Entrepreneurship Trainer and Coach etc. Since 10 June 2018, he has been working aggressively for the welfare and growth of the direct selling industry by training with and consulting for direct sellers and direct selling companies across the globe. More than 10 lakh people from 100 different countries are actively following his work on social media. He is an international master NLP practitioner and has got training from the world's best trainers and leaders in the USA, Singapore, Europe, Bangkok and India.

A master of personal transformation, Deepak has been on a mission to inspire and empower people to be the best they can be for the last 2 decades. Deepak is an expert in human behavior and success psychology who not only delivers insights, tools and strategies but also works deep on people's beliefs and emotions to bring instant change and lasting transformation. Millions of people from 100-plus countries have been achieving their dreams faster with his books, live events, online courses and videos.

Deepak's live events always run with a full house in the thousands because of their powerful international content, unique NLP-based methodology, activity-based interactive learning style and real-life tools and techniques that give instant results and lasting transformation to its participants. More than 11 lakh people have already attended his training sessions. He is a regular keynote speaker at various events and is looked upon as the lighthouse of the direct selling industry. He is also a consultant for many leading companies, helping them multiply their sales and performance.

Direct sellers from all leading companies across the world consider Deepak's online courses as the most trusted and fastest way to achieve results.

Deepak is an avid reader, world traveler and adventure sports enthusiast.

Deepak's life mission is to empower people to be the best they can be. His greatest joy comes from seeing people fulfill their dreams. Deepak and his entire team have been constantly working on creating tools, online courses and events that can help people achieve their goals faster.

You can stay connected with Deepak on various social media platforms and find out more about him and his work at **www.deepakbajaj.biz**.

Table of Contents

Dedication .... *v*

Feedback for Deepak's Books and Courses .... *vii*

Deepak Bajaj's Direct Selling Journey .... *xi*

Why Should You Read This Book? 3

Chapter 1
9 Areas of Your Business Where Social Media 13
Can Help

Chapter 2
7 False Beliefs That Have Been Stopping You From 21
Making It Big With Social Media

Chapter 3
Never Break These 10 Cardinal Rules of Social Media 29

Chapter 4
The 5-Step IDCSR Model To Build Your 39
Personal Brand

Chapter 5
How To Set Up Your Profile in the Right Way 51

Chapter 6
How To Post Like a Pro 59

Chapter 7
The 11-Point System for Creating Never-Ending 73
Content

Chapter 8
    How To Maximize Your Impact and Gain New   83
    Followers Organically

Chapter 9
    Choosing the Right Social Media Platform for You   99

Chapter 10
    11 Strategies for Creating Engaging and Eye-Catching   111
    Posts

Chapter 11
    14 Expert Secrets for Making Impactful Videos on a   121
    Low Budget

Chapter 12
    Secret Formulas of the World's Best Leaders and   137
    Social Media Influencers

Chapter 13
    The Social Media Sales Funnel for Generating   147
    Never-Ending Business Online

Chapter 14
    15 Principles and Strategies for Online Business   159
    Multiplication

Chapter 15
    Use Social Media, but Don't Let It Use You – 5 Traps   173
    To Avoid

The Next Steps   179

Deepak Bajaj's High-Performance Solutions for Life   183
and Business Excellence

Acknowledgements   *187*

ATTENTION PLEASE

This is not a regular book to be read and put back on the shelf. It's your life and business playbook.

This book has been meticulously designed for results and transformation. It has been loaded with hundreds of tools and strategies that you can quickly apply to witness instant results. Almost 2 decades of my experiences of training and consulting more than 10 lakh people have been distilled for you in this book in the form of ideas and insights that are easy to understand and practical to use.

    Every chapter has got a summary and key tasks at the end. There is space after every chapter for marking your action points. If you need more help, you can join my community through my website and social media accounts; I regularly share the latest insights and strategies absolutely free of cost. My intention is not only to give you knowledge but also to make you a master of these concepts so that you get real results.

    This book will serve as your business playbook or workbook that you can use every day to totally transform your life and business. I am super excited that we will improve your game with every chapter.

Why Should You Read This Book?

"We don't have a choice on whether we do social media; the question is how well we do it."

— Erik Qualman

WE HUMANS ARE SOCIAL beings that survive and thrive with mutual connection. We are born with this natural instinct to connect with others, and this connection with others makes us feel happy and secure. Social networking platforms have utilized this basic human instinct to bring the world together on social media. What started as a small initiative has already connected almost half of the world population.

As per an article published by the Statista Research Department on statista.com on 29 June 2021, 3.78 billion out of 8 billion people in the world will be connected on social media by 2021. A quick look at Illustration 1 will show that Facebook alone has 2.7 billion (279 crore) active users, followed by YouTube with 2.29 billion (229 crore) active users.

Another article published by the Statista Research Department on statista.com on 28 June 2021 shows that India alone has 33 crore active Facebook users followed by the USA, Indonesia and Brazil with 19, 14 and 13 crore active Facebook users respectively. If Facebook India were a country, it would rank number 3 in terms of world population.

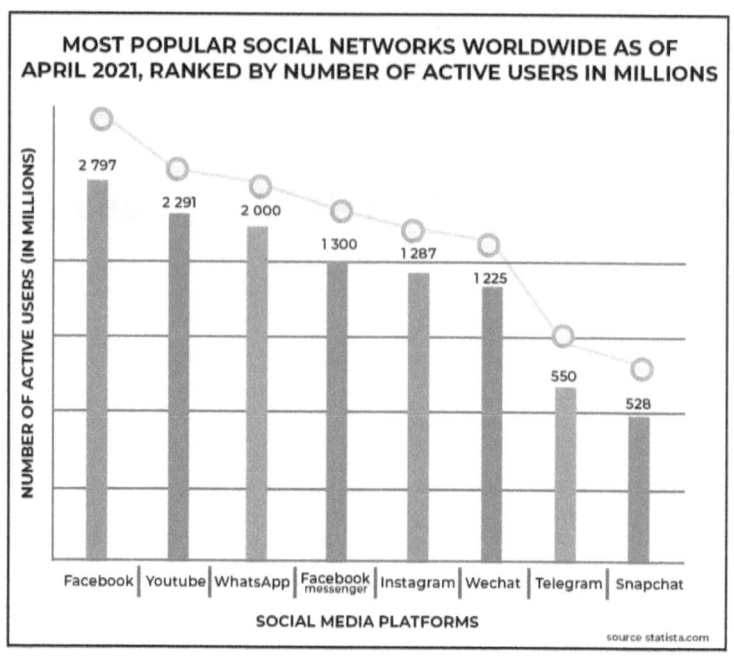

Illustration 1 *

At the same time, it's not just teenagers who are using social media; it's spread across all age groups. While 90% of people between the ages of 18-29 in the USA are actively using social media, 40% of people above the age of 65 are also using social media, and these numbers are growing by the second (source: Statista Research Department on statista.com). A similar trend is expected in all other countries as well.

A massive rise in smartphone penetration has further fueled this social media growth. As per an article published by S. O'Dea on 31 March 2021 on statista.com, 3.6 billion people across the globe have been using smartphones in 2020 and this number is expected to rise to 4.3 billion by 2023. China is the number 1 country in the world in terms of the number of

---

*   Source: https://www.statista.com/statistics/272014/global-social-networks-ranked-by-number-of-users/

smartphone users followed by India, the USA, Indonesia and Brazil.

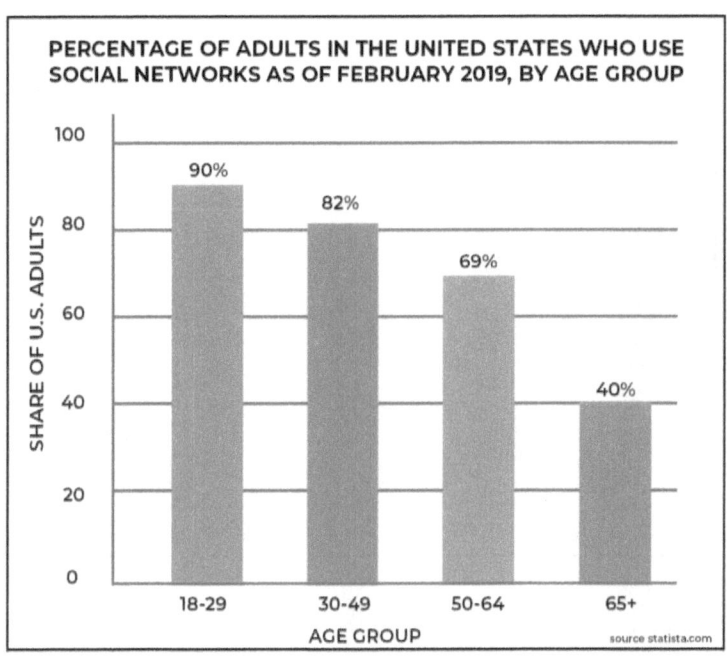

Illustration 2*

While India has the second highest number of smartphone users in the world, what is interesting to note is that India still ranks at number 19 in terms of smartphone penetration (see Illustration 3). While only 31.8% of India's total population has been using smartphones, this number is standing at 81.6% for the USA, 63% for China and 58.6% for Indonesia. In the same report, India was ranked at #40 in 2018, #45 in 2017 and #47 in 2013. Looking at this trend, it is very clear that India will witness a huge rise in the number of smartphone users in the coming few years and with such a rise, the number of social media users will also multiply significantly.

---

*   Source: https://www.statista.com/statistics/471370/us-adults-who-use-social-networks-age/

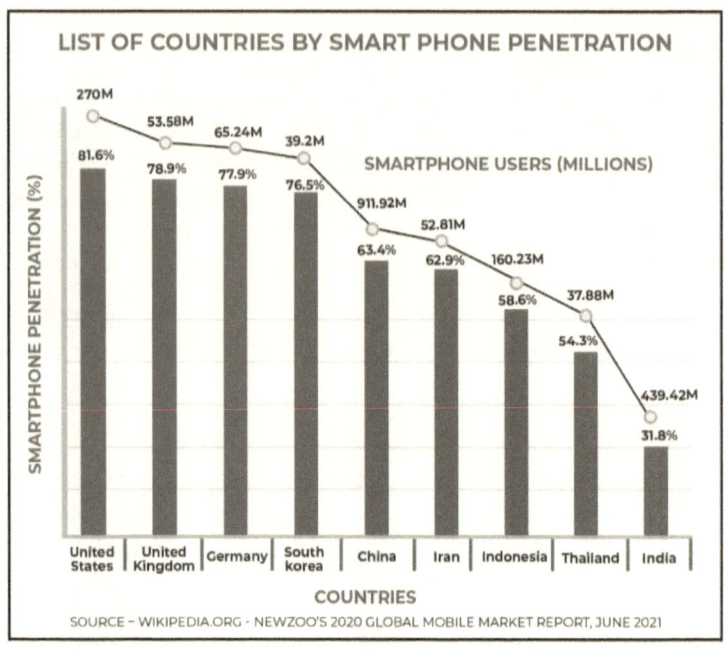

Illustration 3 *

> "Social media is here. It's not going away. Not a passing fad. Be where your customers are: in social media."
>
> — Lori Ruff

The whole world has shifted online and it is said that businesses that are not online will soon be out of business. What is true for any other business is true for direct selling too. Your social media account is your address. People first look at your social media account before they make the decision to do business with you. Your social media accounts are your first impression and people make a lot of judgments about you by looking at your social media account.

But it is interesting to note that social media is the most incredible and, unfortunately, the most disastrous thing that

---

* https://en.wikipedia.org/wiki/List_of_countries_by_smartphone_penetration

has happened to direct selling. It took the smart direct sellers to the next level by empowering them to connect with and prospect an unlimited number of quality prospects globally, while taking the majority of amateurs to new lows as they annoyed and spammed the masses, thereby spoiling the reputation of the industry.

Actually, people got a new toy in the form of social media and they started playing with it by doing all kinds of crazy experiments. Simply put – my goal for this book is to change the way people in the direct selling business utilize what is definitely the most powerful recruiting, brand-building and business multiplication tool ever invented in the history of this world. This book aims to transform you and your business by empowering you with the skills and tools necessary for building a big direct selling business online by utilizing the potential of social media. This book will not only teach you social media management but it will also train you on social media in a way that multiplies your success while elevating the profession of direct selling. I love and respect the direct selling industry and two of my life missions are:

1. To bring pride and glory to the profession of direct selling.
2. To inspire and train direct sellers to succeed bigger and faster.

I am sure this book will help in achieving both of these goals. This book aims to make you succeed faster while uplifting the profession of direct selling.

The tragedy is, most of direct sellers look at social media as if it were a dartboard on which you can just throw darts in the hope that something will hit the mark and you will succeed. People keep wasting years on social media in the hope that someone will respond or buy their products. Most of the darts never hit the mark and some people quit in frustration. Please remember that hope is not a strategy. You need to work with goals and not hope.

Some people feel that they are making progress or building their brand, but that's only an illusion. 99% of direct sellers don't even know what to post or how to post it. In fact, most of the people spoil their name and the reputation of the direct selling industry with whatever they post. Some others are happy just by looking at the number of likes, views or followers they have. But the good news is that there are proven strategies for building your social media brand and I am going to teach you the same in this book.

Remember, there are as many ways to work on social media as there are people. Many social media influencers and digital marketers have been teaching paid promotions and other complicated strategies with which to grow social media accounts. Those strategies may be good but are not duplicable. I also had the option to make it complicated, but I decided to teach you concepts that are easy to implement and at the same time are easily duplicable, because I know that anything that is not duplicable, however good it may be, is a total disaster in direct selling.

I can talk about fancy stuff like building funnels, Facebook advertisements, webinars, SEO, Google ads, squeeze pages, free downloads, automation, having your own URL, having your own website, email automation, campaigns, free products, paid advertisements etc. But truly speaking, none of these are necessary for building an ever-growing direct selling business with speed, stability and a solid foundation. You can earn lakhs of rupees in passive income every month by implementing the simple concepts that I have shared in this book. You need not hire staff or an agency or spend lakhs of rupees in paid promotions to implement the ideas that you will learn in this book.

The number one problem that 99% of direct sellers complain about is that they have exhausted their prospect list. Please remember, 33 crore Indians are active users of Facebook as of 2021. The problem is not that your list has been exhausted; the real problem is that you have still not found a system to tap into this huge unexplored market. Be it list expansion, prospecting, sales closing, retaining your team, establishing your leadership or building your brand, if used in the right way, social media can solve most, if not all, of these problems. If you master the right principles and techniques for using social media, you will become unstoppable in this business, and that is exactly what this book aims to do for you.

What you are holding in your hands is a no-nonsense book that is full of ideas and strategies that I have already implemented myself and got unbelievable results from. Thousands of our course participants across the globe have already got amazing results by using these strategies. There are no complicated theories or jargon, only solutions that are simple to understand and easy to implement.

During my experience training and consulting with more than 11 lakh people in the last 14 years, I have mastered the process of success psychology and personal transformation that brings instant results and lasting transformation. All my experience and insights have been distilled into this book to deliver you incredible results. This is not just a book, it is a complete manual for you to achieve massive success.

> *"Ignoring social media and online marketing is like opening a business but never telling anyone about it."*
> — Anonymous

The rules of the game have totally changed in the last few years and COVID-19 has further sped up the process. Now you can either change or perish. You cannot stop these changes, but you can learn how to operate with these new rules and create success for yourself like you have never achieved before.

This is the best time in the history of the world to build a direct selling business. I don't know which stage you are in – whether you have a social media account or not, how many views or likes you get, how many followers you already have, how much business you are getting from social media, what the current situation of your business is or what your goals are, but I know one thing for sure – what you are holding in your hands is the complete social media mastery manual. If you are willing to learn and implement what you read in this book, you will surprise yourself with what you can achieve.

Stay connected and continue sharing your success stories and experiences.

All my love, strength and wishes for you.

— **Deepak Bajaj**

HOW TO GET MAXIMUM RESULTS FROM THIS BOOK

- Key takeaways have been given at the end of the every chapter. Reviewing them, implementing them, discussing them with others and sharing the same on your social media accounts is a sure shot way to deeply internalize those concepts.
- Every chapter has some recommended actions for you to enhance your results. Please complete those actions.
- Social media is a skill that you develop at the speed of your implementation. So implement every idea that you will learn from this book.

Sources used:

- https://www.statista.com/statistics/467163/forecast-of-smartphone-users-in-india/
- statista.com/statistics/330695/number-of-smartphone-users-worldwide/

CHAPTER 1

9 Areas of Your Business Where Social Media Can Help

"Technology and social media have brought power back to the people."
— Mark McKinnon

SINCE THE INCEPTION OF the direct selling business in the 1940s, direct sellers have been struggling with 4 key challenges, and most people quit because they are not able to solve one or more of these challenges:

1. You have exhausted your prospect list
2. People don't start business with you after seeing your presentation
3. People who join your team don't work actively
4. Your teammates quit the business too soon

All those who have found solutions to these challenges have survived and thrived in this business, but a vast majority is still struggling. In 2018, I wrote my first book, *Be a Network Marketing Millionaire*, that has since been recognized as a compulsory guidebook for every direct seller, irrespective of company, product or income plan. This book has been translated into several languages and continues to be the most followed and recommended book in the industry.

In that book, I had written several pages about social media, but little did I know that within 3 years I would be writing a whole book exclusively on using social media to build a direct selling business. The key reason why I chose to write this book is because over a period of time, social media has demonstrated that it has the potential to solve some of these major challenges that direct sellers face. The amazing features and applications of social media can help everyone in building a large direct selling business.

I am also really thrilled with another fact – as I use social media more and more, I continue to find even more ways in which it can help us in achieving our goals and multiplying our impact. Personally, social media has empowered me to impact millions of people across the globe and help transform so many lives with my books, videos, ebooks, online courses, high-performance coaching and live training events. As of writing of this book, I have participants in my online course from 50-plus countries and my social media content is being watched in 100-plus countries. How could I have achieved this without social media?

Actually, the world around us has totally changed over the last few years. People's habits and lifestyles have totally changed. Learning has shifted from the classroom to the internet. Entertainment has moved from television to Netflix and YouTube. Google and Twitter have replaced news channels. Games have moved from playgrounds to mobile phones. In fact, mobile gaming has become one of the biggest and fastest-growing industries in the world. In this scenario, those direct sellers who fail to change themselves and their working style as per the changing trends will fail to survive.

The direct selling business takes place with people. In the past, direct sellers used to contact their prospects at railway stations, weddings, social functions, airports etc. but now, people are always glued to their mobile phones. And what are they doing with their mobile phones? Using social media.

So principally, direct sellers should be there where people are present, and if people have moved to social media, it's essential for direct sellers to also move their business to social media. It's high time that direct sellers work with new tools and strategies for list expansion, prospecting, brand building, sales closing, team management, training etc. using social media and other online tools and technologies.

> *"The key to success is to start before you are ready."*
> — MARIE FORLEO

Half of the world's population is already connected on social media because social media has dissolved boundaries and has made the whole world accessible to anyone at almost zero cost. This book is your preparation to succeed in this ever-changing new world. Everything that you learn in this book will empower you to utilize social media to achieve your dreams faster. Here are some of the benefits that social media offers you:

1. You will attract good-quality prospects

As you grow your social media brand, you will connect with so many different people and your prospect list will continue to grow. Not only will you get an unlimited number of prospects, but you will also be able to choose the best prospects to share your business with. The right prospects will start contacting you instead of you approaching them. As your content travels to unknown people, you will be able to build a never-ending pipeline of quality prospects.

2. Your sales conversion ratio will multiply

Most people will look at your social media accounts before making the decision to join you. A good social media account will make it easier for your prospects to trust you, thereby increasing your sales conversion ratio. A better sales conversion ratio simply means more results for the same efforts.

3. Retention of people is easier

Everyone loves to be with a growing leader. Your social media account is an excellent platform to showcase your achievements and leadership. Why would your teammates leave when they know they are with a good leader?

4. Your team will perform better

Doubts and confusion kill productivity and performance. People always feel secure with a good leader. Your teammates will perform better when they trust that they are in good hands. Every post on your social media account gives reassurance to your team that they have an active, strong and growing leader to back them. This confidence multiplies their performance.

5. Personal sponsoring is easier

Personal sponsoring is the core of the direct selling business. This quote from my book, *Be a Network Marketing Millionaire*, summarizes the power of personal sponsoring:

> *"Everyone starts his or her direct selling career with personal sponsoring. Those who make it to the top 1% in the industry simply continue doing it years after they had started."*
>
> — Deepak Bajaj

Social media builds your brand in such a way that you attract the best-quality prospects, your sales closing is better and your achievements are constantly reaching out to an unknown audience. All this empowers you for constant personal sponsoring. With every new person that you sponsor, you will grow your width and depth, thereby multiplying your income.

6. Constant list expansion

Social media has brought the whole world to you. People are now just a post or a video away from you. You never know where your posts or videos will reach. Friends of friends, recommended posts, suggestions, shares and platform algorithms can take your posts to unknown people within seconds. As your circle of influence multiplies on social media, so will your list.

My first book, *Be a Network Marketing Millionaire*, was doing well since its launch in 2018. It is the first of its kind – a book that has the complete information, tools, insights and strategies that people need for building a big direct selling business. The value this book added to people's lives was amazing and many saw amazing results. But despite all this, my readership was limited to people who already knew me or their immediate circle. Then I started my YouTube channel and started talking about my book in some of my YouTube videos. As people started sharing my videos, the readership of my book also went through the roof. So however good you may be, it will not get you what you deserve until your message reaches the masses, and social media can spread your message at lightning speed.

> *"The best known will replace the best."*
> — DEEPAK BAJAJ

7. Constant communication with your friends and followers

Every post that you share will remind people about you and your work. You can make an unlimited number of new friends. You can stay connected and up-to-date with everyone you've known, from your childhood to today, through your social media profile. One of the biggest challenges is to maintain constant communication with people and social media is a great way to stay in touch with an infinite number of people at the same time. Every post is doing your prospecting for you.

8. Big fame

Social media has brought many YouTubers and Instagram influencers on par with several Bollywood and Hollywood celebrities. People who were unknown to the world a few years ago are enjoying followerships in the millions today only because of their social media accounts. They are endorsing brands and earning money like crazy. I am not asking you to become an influencer on social media, but as you grow your business and social media accounts, your achievements will reach wider audiences and your fame will multiply. You will become a sought-after leader. When you go for business conferences, all those people who follow you on social media will come looking for you and take selfies with you and ask you for autographs. If you do it right, your social media accounts can become your ticket to stardom.

9. Multiplies the impact of your speech and training

Social media multiplies your leadership and influence. Done properly, every post and video builds up your image and reputation. It enhances your credibility and gives more weight to your words. I am not saying that just posting things without the achievements to back them up will build up your leadership. I am assuming that you are following the principles of the business and doing everything it takes to build a big business. But I have seen that many times, good work was lost because it didn't reach the right people. Social media can showcase and highlight your achievements to your team and when they see you growing, they will respect you more and follow your action plans.

As per datareportal.com, on average, 16 new users join social media every single second, and a typical user actively uses or visits 6 or more different social media platforms every month and spends close to 2½ hours on different social media platforms every day.* Assuming people sleep for 7-8 hours every day, these figures suggest that people spend, on average, 15 percent of their waking hours on social media.

Social media has gradually become a part of our culture and it's here to stay and grow. It is going to become more interactive and technologically advanced. People will find more creative ways for effective communication and for getting better results. It is definitely going to be a key determinant of success in the future. I have mentioned 9 key areas where social media has already started helping direct sellers, but I am sure that with the passage of time and more technological advancements, these benefits will multiply. Social media is a tool and it purely depends on your creativity as to where you use it and the benefits you reap from it.

> *"The great thing about social media was how it gave a voice to voiceless people."*
>
> — JON RONSON

---

* https://datareportal.com/social-media-users

REMEMBER AND SHARE

- What social media can do for you is infinite; the only limit is your imagination.
- Direct selling is all about people, and direct sellers should be present where people are present. Since people have moved to social media, it would be wise for direct sellers to move there as well – and urgently.
- New winning combination for success = network marketing benefits and principles + social media + online tools.
- If you want a never-ending pipeline of prospects, you should work on developing a system that continues to add names to your list even when you are sleeping.
- Your sales conversion ratio is in direct proportion to your brand value.
- Building your social media accounts will not only help you attract the right people but will also help you retain your teammates.

KEY ACTIONS TO TAKE

- Post your top 3 learnings from this chapter on your social media accounts.
- List down the areas of your work where social media can help you.

CHAPTER 2

7 False Beliefs That Have Been Stopping You From Making It Big With Social Media

"If you believe you can, you probably can. If you believe you won't, you most assuredly won't. Belief is the ignition switch that gets you off the launching pad."

— Denis Waitley

I HAVE A VERY POPULAR course for direct sellers called *Social Media and Online Business Mastery*. Tens of thousands of direct sellers from across the globe have already transformed their lives with that course. One of my course participants from Canada asked me this question: "When social media is so accessible and offers so many amazing benefits, why don't most people use it for building their business?"

Here is what I answered: "While many people are struggling due to a lack of the right knowledge and techniques, there is a large majority who are stuck because of their own false beliefs. After training more than 10 lakh people, I have realized that the biggest battles are fought in our minds. Several conflicting thoughts and emotions constantly run through our minds and this constant conflict deprives us from taking full benefit of the amazing tool of social media."

I want to make utilizing social media as easy for you as brushing your teeth and this will happen when we change these 7 false beliefs that I am going to discuss in this chapter.

False Belief #1
"I can build a big business even without social media."

Yes, you definitely can. Social media is not compulsory. It's a tool that can make your life easier and can help you reach out to the masses right from your phone. It can make you more efficient and save you a lot of time and money. Just like any other tool, you always have the option to use it and if so, how much to use it.

You are free to say that you can manage without social media, but how will you respond when your teammates and new prospects ask you questions like, "Why don't you have a good social media account?" Or, "How can we answer this question on social media?" Or, "How do you do list expansion or prospecting on social media?"And so on. Some of you must already be facing similar questions from your children or younger teammates. Today, social media and online business-building tools may appear optional, but within a few years they will become an essential part of our business-building model, by which time they will be even more difficult to learn. COVID-19 has already taught us this invaluable lesson.

I have realized that many people who say that they will build a big business without using social media are those who have spent many months on social media but never gotten any results, or those who are scared because they don't know how to approach it in the right way. I highly recommend that you complete this book and set off. I am sure that you will have a different experience this time. If you feel the need, you could also take up some online course that could shorten your learning time.

False Belief #2

"I need a large account to take advantage of social media."

Having worked with lakhs of participants from my online courses and live events across the globe, I can tell you this with absolute certainty: *"It's not the size of the account but the quality and consistency of the account that brings results."*

Everyone knows that subscribers and views can be bought, but not the quality, consistency and connection to the audience. Your social media account is your address and it showcases what you do and how you do it. People will follow you and stay connected to you only because of you and your work. Ask yourself – do you follow someone because of the number of followers they have or because of who they are and what they share?

You need to dissociate the number of followers on a social media account from the business that it generates. These are two entirely different things. I know hundreds of people with big social media accounts that are generating zero or negligible business. At the same time, I personally know thousands of my own courses' students who are generating massive business with small accounts.

Remember your why. Why are you going to social media? If you want to be a social media influencer, then the number of followers may matter. But if your goal is to build a big direct selling business, simply implement what you are going to learn in the next few pages and you will thank me very soon for the business results that you will get.

> *"Social networks aren't about websites.*
> *They are about experiences."*
> — MIKE DILORENZO

False Belief #3
"Paid advertisements and digital marketing are necessary for success."

This is totally false. In fact, the biggest mistake you will ever make with your direct selling business would be to use paid advertisements or complicated digital marketing sales funnels. These are not wrong but are just not duplicable for your team. The core principles of direct selling are simplicity, ease of doing for anyone, anywhere and no marketing expenses. That's how you build a team of independent leaders and a passive income model.

I started my direct selling business on 28 June 2007. I had an awesome start and a big income right from the first month due to my excellent selling skills and commitment. But after four months, my business started going down and crashed to zero. It took me 9 months to bring it back, but those months of struggling and the daily financial challenges taught me much more than years of success. I rebuilt my organization from the ground up with such a powerful system and tools that from January 2009, I started earning passive income from the business.

I bought my first Mercedes-Benz in 2009, followed by a collection of cars, houses, investments, foreign trips to 27 countries and a totally transformed lifestyle. What brought all these things into my life was not my personal skills or talents but a powerful system. I later realized the same applied for the thousands of my course participants and live event trainees – that you don't need paid advertisements or a special talent for lakhs of rupees in passive income. All you need is a proven and duplicable system, and that's what I train people to develop.

Someone once asked me during an interview – "Direct selling is such a simple business; why do you work with people for 91 days in your online course, *Ultimate Network*

Marketing Mastery?" I replied, "Basic selling skills can be taught in a few hours, but if you want to build a real passive income generating model that will continue to give you income, happiness, respect and impact generation after generation, you need a powerful total transformation system of mindset, skillset and toolset, and that's what I instill in people in 91 days. Anyone can do training but what really matters are results and transformation."

You can simply follow the principles that are taught in this book and you will not need to spend a single rupee in paid promotions.

False Belief #4
"It's too late for me to start now."

This is just an excuse you are giving yourself. What is social media? It's a place to connect and engage with like-minded people. How can anyone be late for creating connections with others? What you do on social media is exactly what people have been doing since the birth of mankind. Connecting with others is a human need. Even though there are already 3.7 billion people on social media as of my writing this book, there is no other you. You are the power of your brand. Social media is a platform to celebrate your uniqueness. Throw away all these false beliefs and just get there. So many people need you and your unique gifts. Go all out and share your gifts with the world.

> *"You don't have to be great to start,*
> *but you have to start to be great."*
> — Zig Ziglar

False Belief #5
"I am not good at connecting with people."

Nobody was born with the skill to connect with people. Every expert started as an amateur one day. Any skill can be learned as long as you have the desire and commitment to learn it. I'm sure that you have the desire – that's why you are reading this book. Get started and remember, progress is perfection.

False Belief #6
"I can't put my personal life in front of the world."

Who told you to put your personal life in front of the world? There is no such rule. It's your social media account and you decide what to put and what not to put on your account. Set your own rules. Be yourself and do what you find comfortable. I share only what I feel like sharing on my social media account. I don't post every single photo that I click during the day. It's purely my choice and I am happy with that. Begin with what you feel is right and you will evolve as you start using social media.

False Belief #7
"I don't look good or talk well or have much to show."

If you are planning to go to social media to impress people, you have lost the game before you have even started. Social media is the place not to impress people but to connect with people and build your tribe. Let me repeat: the world wants to see you and connect with you. If you want to fake things on social media, you will be stressed all the time and social media will become just another punishment or boring chore for you. We all want you as you are. What matters the most is your intention to add value and serve your community.

I can tell you from my personal experience that social media is a great place to get good feedback. As you observe your own videos, photos or content, you will start noticing areas of your personality that you may want to improve. You can also get genuine feedback from people that can help you grow. Social media can become a transformational journey for you.

Honestly speaking, these are some of the myths or false beliefs that I have also faced myself. I don't know what has been stopping you. But I can assure you of one thing – that you are stronger than you think you are, and you are enough. Don't wait for inspiration or things to be in a certain way. Just start from wherever you are and with whatever you have. As you move forward, you will start seeing the road ahead. I invite you to start walking, because some answers will be revealed to you only after you start taking action.

> *"Social media is the ultimate equalizer. It gives a voice and a platform to anyone willing to engage."*
>
> — Amy Jo Martin

REMEMBER AND SHARE

- Social media is a wonderful tool to multiply your business but the final decision on how to use it and to what extent lies entirely with you. Set your rules and get started.
- If you have not got results from social media in the past, it is most likely because of the way you approached it. If you use the right principles and techniques, you will certainly get the desired results. Learn them.
- It's not the number of followers but the connections and engagement that bring results from your social media account.
- If you don't know how to use social media, then the solution is to learn the same and not shrink away from it.
- Don't go to social media to impress people, go there to connect with people.

KEY ACTIONS TO TAKE

- If you have not yet got the results you deserve from social media, identify what could have gone wrong – belief, efforts, techniques or content. Once you have identified the problem, work on making it right.

CHAPTER 3

Never Break These 10 Cardinal Rules of Social Media

"You have to learn the rules of the game and then you have to play better than anyone else."
— DIANNE FEINSTEIN

SOMEONE RIGHTLY SAID THAT anything worth doing is worth doing well. So if you have decided to use social media for your personal branding and business growth, why not do it the right way? Just like any other field, social media has certain fixed rules and your success can be faster and easier if you work with these rules. Even if you want to break the rules, you should know the rules first. So here are the 10 cardinal rules of social media.

#1. Don't look for immediate results from every post

Do you expect a stranger to start business with you just by looking at you? Of course not. We understand that there is a process from the beginning of the relationship to making someone a business partner. It's the same with social media. You post something and people look at it. You can't expect people to develop a liking and trust for you just by looking at your first few posts. So many people who started business with me told me that they have silently observed me for almost a year before deciding to do so.

If you are looking for immediate results from every single post, you have not understood the philosophy behind social media. Social media is a long-term game because every post is like a seed and you never know where it will reach and what it will do for you.

You are here to build your brand, and you don't build your brand on what you occasionally do; rather, you build your brand on what you do consistently over a period of time. People and social media algorithms start taking you seriously after 3-6 months of consistent effort. But once you are able to take up your social media account to a certain level, it will continue to work for you even when you are not working. A well-developed social media account will become your round-the-clock assistant.

1st Instagram post
5th Jan 2018
73 Likes

Another Instagram Post
17th Dec 2019
30814 Likes

#2. People come to social media to socialize and not for shopping

Have you ever felt the need to buy toothpaste and decide to go to Facebook to buy it? Have you seen anyone who wants to buy a book who goes to Instagram to shop for one? Nobody does it and you know it is stupid, but you will still notice a majority of direct sellers making the mistake of trying to sell products on social media every single day.

People post 10 pictures of their product, testimonies, videos and company conferences and loudly write everywhere – "Buy this", "Buy that", "Join me", "Our company is the best", "Join early for more benefits", "Newest opportunity in the market" etc. Do you think people follow and buy from such idiots? Never. If you are posting pictures of your products and make posts seeking people to join you, this is called advertising and not posting. Never, ever forget this rule – people come to social media to meet people, to connect and to socialize; never to buy. Respect people and you will get much more than you could ever imagine.

> "Social media is about the people. Not about your business. Provide for the people and the people will provide for you."
> — MATT GOULART

#3. Don't try to be everywhere

Some people feel that opening accounts on different social media platforms is like collecting trophies, and they are always in this race to become the first one in their circle to have an account on anything new that comes up. Yes, it's free and it is tempting to open and operate your social media account on all the platforms in the hope that a different set of people may recognize you there. But the fact remains that the amount of business you will get from social media depends not on the number of accounts you operate but on the connection and engagement you have with your followers on any account. Getting engagement is serious work that requires time, commitment and consistency. Starting something is easy but maintaining consistency is tough, and algorithms operate on consistency. Also, it is exhausting to create unique content every day for different platforms.

Anyway, there are more social media platforms than you or I can imagine, and I am not writing any number here because by the time this book reaches you, the number would have grown substantially from what it is today. So it's not humanly possible for anyone to be present everywhere. I recommend you build your base with 1-2 platforms that you are most comfortable with and gradually expand to more if you feel the need. Have patience and build a loyal audience by providing consistent value. Also, once you have built any one good social media account, it starts attracting new audiences and gives a good first impression of you.

#4. A + C + C = R

This one formula should serve as your guiding light while working on social media.

$$A + C + C = R$$
Attention + Connection + Consistency = Results

Everything that I have shared in this book has been designed to empower you to work with this formula. We will discuss more about this as we go along but for now, please understand that your key task on social media is to grab the attention of your target audience with great posts and build a connection with them. You can start expecting results only after you have been doing it consistently for a long period of time.

#5. Don't follow everyone and don't believe everything you see

One of the main reasons for the exponential rise of social media is that it's free and anyone can post anything. But this biggest advantage sometimes becomes its biggest disadvantage. There are no checks on who is posting something and what is being posted. That responsibility and judgment has been left entirely to you.

So you should be very careful of whom you follow. Everyone is claiming to be a coach or consultant these days. Check to see if they have done what they are teaching. Are you following a genuine person or some fake coach created by paid advertisements and digital marketing? Don't believe every piece of information shared on social media. Check for the authenticity of the source. Whatever you allow to go inside your mind will show its effect sooner or later. Make sure anything that will not help you does not get inside your head. It's your mind, not a dustbin.

Remember: social media is free, but your time and energy are priceless.

#6. Social media is part of the strategy and not the whole strategy

Don't ever forget that you are using social media to achieve your business objectives and not to become a social media influencer. For a direct seller, social media is just a part of the strategy and not the whole strategy. So decide your time slots and the number of minutes you will devote to it every day and stick to it. Don't be under the illusion that spending more time on social media will result in more business.

#7. Social media will never replace face-to-face meetings

During one live event someone asked me, "Which one is better – online business or offline?" If you are a student of any of my online programs you must be familiar with my 'answer questions with questions' technique. I replied, "Which one is more important – eyes or ears?" The person was taken aback for a bit but quickly realized the answer.

One-to-one meetings, big events, live training, home meetings, counseling etc. will continue to be there forever. Social media gives you new leverage and offers new opportunities to reach out and stay connected with a large number of people. But social media is not a replacement for offline work; rather, it complements offline fieldwork and events.

During my private mentorship group training, one of the course participants from Australia asked me, "What percentage of our efforts should be online?" Please understand my reply as it can give you a good perspective as you gradually start taking your business online: "We are in the people business and we have two key goals in this business. The first one is to look for the best people to share our opportunity with. Once people become a part of our team, our second goal is to maintain communication with them, nurture the relationships and help them achieve their goals. We should work towards these two goals using all online and offline mediums. There is no fixed ratio. The ultimate objective is to effectively achieve our goals and maximize our impact for the least effort."

#8. Nothing goes unnoticed on social media

Never, ever forget that social media is a public platform. However private and guarded you keep your profile, anything you post on social media is public. You may regret it later but you cannot take it back.

Everything you post, write or share is being noticed by your followers as well as unknown people. Nothing you post is neutral – it either uplifts your brand or downgrades it. So be very careful.

As a general rule, I recommend you avoid talking about sex, politics and religion. Used well, you can use social media to effectively build your personal brand; not used well, it can spoil your reputation. If people can decide to join you by seeing your social media accounts, they can also decide to stay away from you after looking at your social media accounts.

> *"Don't say anything online that you wouldn't want plastered on a billboard with your face on it."*
> — ERIN BURY

#9. Know what to track

Never be in the race to get more views or likes. When you consistently share good content, likes and comments are bound to come. But at the same time, always remember that likes and views on your post depend on many factors apart from you and your content, like what was trending at the time, how the algorithms were operating, what others have posted, what time you posted it, whether it was a holiday or a non-holiday, if anything big happened in the country or the world at the time and probably a hundred other reasons.

As of writing of this book, I have 370-plus videos on my YouTube channel. Each of the videos have been made after doing a lot of research on the content and doing the best possible editing, but every video has still performed differently. There have been videos with 10 lakh-plus views and next to those you will find a video with only 50,000 views. There have been times when I worked extra hard for some particular video and I was sure it would get an amazing response, as my audience had demanded a video on that topic and my team had done the best editing with the necessary software, but the video performed miserably in terms of all general parameters. During my initial days on YouTube, I used to get pretty upset about it.

But gradually, I have made peace with it and have deeply internalized the idea that my goal is to consistently create the best possible content that will help serve my audience. The real game is to consistently grow yourself and your understanding of your audience. Don't let the numbers distract you from producing excellent-quality content that will add consistent value to your audience.

#10. It's not about your company; it's about you

This is the most common mistake direct sellers are making on social media. It is the biggest blunder that amateur direct sellers are making, thereby spoiling their name and the reputation of the direct selling industry. However great your company is and however much you love it, it will never give you any benefit if you always talk about your company on your social media account. Your followers have come to your page for you and not for your company. If they want to connect with your company or products, they will go to your company's page and not yours.

Remember what I told you in my other book, *Be a Network Marketing Millionaire* – people never join a company, people join people. Social media is all about people and all about you. We will explore this topic more in the chapter on personal branding and posting but for now do remember to keep your page yours.

Along with these 10 cardinal rules for social media, always remember the fundamental principle that just doing anything will never give you results; doing right things in the right way is the only way to get massive results. So be committed to following these 10 cardinal rules and accelerate your success.

> "Engage, enlighten, encourage and especially just be yourself! Social media is a community effort; everyone is an asset."
> — SUSAN COOPER

REMEMBER AND SHARE

- Social media is a long-term game. Stay consistent. Social media algorithms start recommending your posts to an unknown audience after noticing your consistency.
- Never forget that people come to social media to meet people, to connect and to socialize; never to buy.
- Don't worry about likes or followers. Achieve your goals with engagement, conversations and connection.
- Posts are different from advertisements. Know what you are posting and what it will do to your reputation.
- The amount of business you will get from social media depends not on the number of accounts you operate, but on the connection and engagement you have with your followers on any account.
- It's not about your company; it's about you.

KEY ACTIONS TO TAKE

- Analyze the key mistakes you have been making on social media in the past.
- Identify 3 key principles from this chapter that you will follow while operating on social media.
- If you got some useful insight from this chapter, share it with your friends on social media.

CHAPTER 4

The 5-Step IDCSR Model To Build Your Personal Brand

"Your brand is what other people say about you when you are not in the room."

— JEFF BEZOS

I HAVE BEEN FASCINATED WITH the concept of branding right from my MBA college days in 2001-03. I was always curious to know how two products in the same industry, both made in the same country and with almost the same cost of production, utility and features were sold at totally different prices and got a completely different response in the same market. While one had to be pushed aggressively; people were queuing up to buy the other one at double the price. What was the difference? Branding.

A brand is the biggest leverage any person or business can have. Have you seen how when some leaders come up to the stage, people give them an endless standing ovation without even asking, while there are many other leaders who get lost in the crowd? What's the difference? Their brand. In fact, my main goal for you with this chapter, with this book and with every online or live event that I do is to empower you to become a leader who not only has the #1 rank and financial freedom but also a big impact, charisma, values and, of course, a unique brand.

A brand is your competitive edge. Anyone can take anything away from you but they cannot be you, and that's your power. That is your brand. A brand is something recognizable that people like or respect. A brand is a set of values that any individual or organization stands for. Once people start associating certain values or qualities with your name, it becomes your brand and it will continue to stay with your name for a long period of time and will give you an edge over everybody else.

Mercedes-Benz, Apple, Rolex, BMW, MS Dhoni, Narendra Modi, Reliance, Amazon, Google, Gucci – these are all brands, and every time you come across one of these names, you immediately think of certain features or qualities that you associate with these brands. What is interesting to note is that branding is not just limited to some features or qualities; rather, it's a deep emotional connection that people have with the brand. Every time you hear a name, you don't just remember their features or qualities; it will also instantly bring out certain emotions in you.

Branding works in every industry and profession. There are leading doctors, lawyers, politicians, teachers, CAs, digital marketers, social media influencers etc. who have made a mark for themselves with their special qualities and the way they have taken up their profession. This has made them special brands in their profession. Whenever somebody is looking for the best person in any profession, guess where they go? People will flock to the professionals with the best brand name. Another big advantage is that once you are able to establish some good values and a reputation with your name, they will continue to stay with you for a longer period of time (provided you don't do anything to spoil your brand).

> "Making promises and keeping them is a great way to build a brand."
>
> — SETH GODIN

I started my direct selling business on 28 June 2007 as a part-time gig along with my job. It was a high-paying, high-pressure job with an automobile MNC but I built this business with such speed and so systematically that within 3 months, my part-time direct selling income surpassed my salary and I resigned my job on 29 Sep 2007. Next month, I achieved the top income level of our company. It was a record performance that had never happened in the many years of that company's history. I started earning passive income from January 2009 and bought my first Mercedes-Benz in 2009. Yes, I earned a big income, lavish lifestyle and recognition, but even more important was the fact that people started associating speed and peak performance with my name. That was the time when the Deepak Bajaj brand was born.

I didn't stop there and continued my direct selling speed rally with one achievement after another. Both of my books became bestsellers within hours of their release. My YouTube channel went from 1,000 to 1,00,000 subscribers in 63 days. My online courses and live events were over-booked and became the most trusted and highest-selling training programs in the direct selling industry. Every achievement made my brand values of speed and top performance stronger and stronger. Now every time people think of Deepak Bajaj, they automatically think of direct selling, speed, training and peak performance, knowing he is a genuine person who teaches what he has done himself. People know Deepak Bajaj's heart and soul is direct selling and every time they think of direct selling, they think of Deepak Bajaj. All this is branding. I mentioned this not to show off my achievements but to demonstrate what the right branding can do for you.

How is a brand made? A brand is built on the basis of our values, beliefs, posts and actions that we demonstrate over a period of time. In simple words, a brand is a label that we put on people, things or companies based on their dominant traits or behavior that they consistently display. Branding is happening all the time. All the people who know you associate certain qualities and traits with your name, but most of it is done unconsciously. Now we want to build your brand consciously in a way that supports you in achieving your personal and business goals faster. That's what I will teach you in this chapter. I want to empower you to establish your brand in such a way that you attract like-minded people and grow your business exponentially.

After studying and working with brands for close to two decades, I have formulated a 5-step IDCSR model for building any brand. Every brand in the world has been built using these 5 steps and you can do it too. Wherever you are and whatever you do, the IDCSR model is very simple to understand and easy to implement. It's so simple that you can start working on this as soon as you finish reading this chapter. Have a quick look at the IDCSR model in Illustration 4 and then we will discuss each of these steps one by one, in detail.

Illustration 4

Step #1. Identify your brand

The first step in building your brand is to identify the set of values and qualities that you want to be associated with your name. Make a conscious decision of what you want to be perceived as and how.

You can do this in two ways – with your passion or your expertise. If you combine these two, it's a jackpot. Think of what you are passionate about. What is the subject or topic that creates a spark in your eyes whenever you start talking about it, that lights up your face and that you can talk endlessly about? You may not be an expert at it but you may still love the subject. It can be anything – reading books, horse riding, yoga, weight loss, entrepreneurship, motivation, lifestyle, wealth, parenting, relationships, food, clothes, movies, fitness, sports, healthy habits, time management, success, fashion, entertainment, travel, social media, digital marketing, YouTube, Instagram, spirituality etc. You can choose any topic of your choice, but if you take up topics like motivation, health coaching, entrepreneurship, wealth coaching, wellness consulting etc., these are too broad and are used by every fifth person in the direct selling industry. Within these areas, find some smaller niche that you want to address – for example, if motivation, then motivation for students or working professionals. Try to find a niche that is unique, or have a unique style for that niche. We want people to associate something specific with your name.

I am asking you to pick up something you are passionate about because you will be talking a lot about this subject every day and there will be times when your audience will be very small in number. You just cannot talk about something endlessly if you are not passionate about it.

> *"Be interesting. Tell the truth. Live your truth."*
>
> — Jonah Sachs

The second route to identify your brand values can be through your expertise. What are you good at? What is your specialization? It may be your degrees, your professional skills or something you have acquired by working on it. You could also combine your passion and expertise if you want.

Now write it down. Be really precise and bring it down to one line. What you have got now is your brand. Read it again – that's what you want to be known for. That's what people should think of when they think of you. That's your core association. This is the value you represent and stand for. You may even identify your own unique way of pursuing your passion. It's not just what you are passionate about doing but also your unique way of doing it that will add value to others. My brand value, for example, is to help direct sellers succeed faster through my unique training methodology and result-delivering tools. Everything I create and do – online programs, live events, books and videos – has been designed with this unique total transformation methodology and is loaded with tools that deliver faster results.

What you have got now is the center around which your life will operate. All your social media posts, actions, talk and behavior will revolve around this central theme. You will live, eat, sleep and breathe this one central idea from now onwards. At this stage, don't worry about questions like who will follow you in this area, whether your brand value is too vague, whether there are already established leaders with the same brand value etc. Just focus on your passion or expertise and start moving forward with this brand value.

Some of you may be curious why I have not included direct selling or network marketing in this list. Please be very clear that we don't want your brand to be network marketing or direct selling. We want it to be something other than direct selling that you are passionate about or good at. You may be wondering how you will recruit people for direct selling if that is not your brand. Don't worry. What we are doing now is not the entire process; it's only the first step of the process. We will do the recruitment at the right time and I will share with you exactly how to do it in the next few pages.

Step #2. Display your brand

After you have clearly identified your brand value, the next logical step is to display it everywhere on your social media page. Everything you write or show on your social media page must display your core brand values. We will discuss the mechanics of setting up your profile in the next chapter but right now, just understand that your profile photo, cover photo, about section, bio, tagline etc. should all be in alignment with your brand.

Your bio or about section is the largest text space you get on your page. It should be a reflection of your brand. You should not solicit people here but should provide all your contact details. Show some energy, fun and passion so that people will love to be around you and stay connected. Please don't forget that your bio or any other display should not look like recruitment advertisements.

Step #3. Communicate your brand

After you have set up your profile and displayed your brand, it's time to go all out and tell the world what you stand for. That's communication, and you will communicate your brand through everything you do and share on social media – posts, quotes, content, videos and live sessions. With every post and video on social media you make, you send a message to the world – who you are, what you stand for, what you stand against and how you intend to add value and serve people.

Step #4. Strengthen your brand

Continue posting for 3-6 months as per your brand value and gradually people will start associating your brand values with your name. That's how you start building your brand. Your brand is not built when you decide your core brand values; rather, your brand is built one day at a time and one post at a time as you consistently add value and serve your audience. As you continue to post around your brand value, people with similar interests will be attracted to your social media profile. People will start interacting with you and start sharing your good content with others. And that's how you will start building your community.

So many influencers and agencies will tell you hundreds of strategies to build your brand but I believe in one strategy that will never fail – **add more value than what your audience expects**. This is a sure shot way to build a loyal following.

> *"Listening is one of the most important things a brand can do online. If your brand is just broadcasting its own agenda, it isn't truly engaging in a conversation."*
>
> — Jeremy Goldman

Step #5. Review the alignment of communication

I have seen lot of people following all the previous 4 steps but over a period of time, unknowingly, whatever they post starts conveying different values than what they originally aimed for. So I highly recommend that once a month, you review your profile like a third party and ask yourself one simple question: *"Are my page and my posts communicating what I stand for and what I intend to communicate?"* If you are not able to do it yourself, take the help of a coach or mentor.

If your answer is yes, then continue whatever you have been doing, but if you feel there is some mismatch, then apply the necessary corrections immediately. It may also be possible that your own definition of your brand will change as you start posting. It's so amazing that many times, we actually realize our true brand values after we start posting about them. I have noticed with many of my high-performance clients that whatever brand values people start with gradually change after a period of time. Don't worry about it; it's a sign of growth.

Now you know all the five steps for building your brand and I am sure you must be excited about starting your brand-building journey. But before you begin, I want to offer you something more – 3 expert secrets from my two decades of experience in handling brands that will help you avoid some of the biggest branding mistakes that I have seen people, especially direct sellers, make repeatedly.

> *"Social media is about sociology and psychology more than technology."*
>
> — Brian Solis

Expert Branding Secret #1. Your brand is about you

I have already told you this and I will probably repeat this again somewhere in this book because this is really important. Never, ever forget that your brand is not about your company or network marketing. Your brand is about you – what you stand for, your passions, your values, what you are against, what drives you etc. People connect with you over something that you are actually passionate about. Once they are connected to you, you can tell them about your network marketing business at the right opportunity, but definitely not in your posts. The rule is simple – first people like you, then they like what you do.

Expert Branding Secret #2. Personal branding is an ongoing process

Always remember that the process of building your social media brand will go parallel to building your direct selling business. Personal branding is not like a crash course that you do for 2-4 weeks, after which you start building a real business. Building your social media brand is a part of building the real business. This is not the first step to building a business but is one of the essential daily activities of building a big business like list expansion, personal sponsoring and business opportunity presentations.

Expert Branding Secret #3. Begin right now

I have seen so many people who understand the IDCSR model but spend days and weeks just in identifying their brand. They are perfectionists who want to be right the very first time. Many of them suffer from a disease called 'paralysis of analysis'. I have explained to you this model so that you can

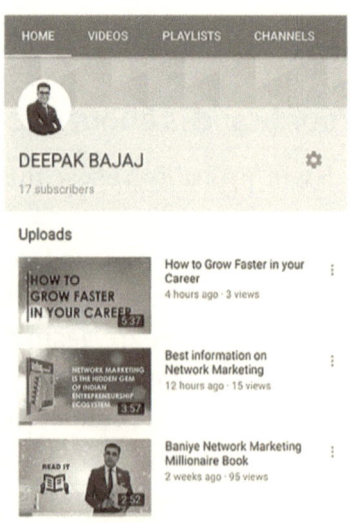

1st Sep 2018   1st Sep 2021

speed up your brand-building process and not just get stuck. Identify your brand value today and whatever you come up with, immediately take action with the next steps. Don't doubt it and don't spend days thinking about it. Just get out there and start talking about things you are passionate about, sharing what you care about, what you stand for or what you know best. Brand building is a journey and you will grow with the process and your true brand will evolve with time. I have been on this transformation journey for 2 decades now and am really excited about what is going to come next.

Before we move forward with the other chapters important for your social media mastery, I want to warn you about one thing in personal branding. While a good act will move you one step forward, a wrong act will pull you back at least 10 steps. People will rarely share the good things that you do but any time you do something wrong, it will be broadcasted like everybody's business. So as you become a brand, your character, choice of words, behavior and integrity will be under a scanner 24/7. So just be careful before you speak, post or do anything.

> *"It takes 20 years to build a reputation and five minutes to ruin it. If you think about that, you will do things differently."*
>
> — Warren Buffet

REMEMBER AND SHARE

- People associate different values and qualities with your name based on what you speak, do and share consistently. That's your brand.
- Branding is a slow process but once established, it will be your biggest advantage.
- What you post about consistently communicates and strengthens your brand.
- Your brand is never about your company or network marketing. It's about you.
- First people like you, then they like what you do.
- Personal branding is an ongoing process. The process of building your social media brand will go parallel to building your network marketing business.

KEY ACTIONS TO TAKE

- Identify and write down your brand value – the key quality that you want to be known for.
- Check if your page is communicating the same value that you want to communicate.
- Redesign your posts and videos based on your brand values.

CHAPTER 5

How To Set Up Your Profile in the Right Way

"It's about your audience. Not you."
— RHEA FREEMAN

YOUR PROFILE IS THE first thing people notice when they come to your page. It's like your showroom, or maybe the entrance to your showroom. Your profile is your first impression and you never get a second chance to make that first impression. When people come to your social media account, they make the decision to follow you or not follow you by looking at your profile for few seconds. So you need to set up your profile in a professional and appealing way and that is what you will learn in this chapter.

Let's understand this with an analogy. How do you go to meetings? Well-dressed, ready, fully equipped and with the best of personal hygiene. The same goes for your profile as well. You need to carefully set it up in such a way that it gives the desired first impression about you and your brand values. One look at your profile and people should know who you are and what you do. When you go about setting your profile, please remember that people are too distracted these days. With hundreds of mobile phone notifications and constant multi-tasking on laptops, you have to meticulously plan every detail of your profile to make it impressive and visually appealing. It should help people make the right judgment about you instantly. You should aim to set up your profile in such a way that people should feel like clicking and knowing more about you and later, becoming a friend or follower.

Like with everything else on social media, there are countless ways to set up your profile and none of them are right or wrong. I would also like you to set up your profile in your own unique way but what I want to share with you today is a set of simple guidelines to help you attract the right people and move your business forward. Add your creativity and your own unique style to whatever you are learning in this book and I am sure you will shine like a diamond.

I hope you remember the KLT rule of selling. This book and all my online programs are designed to empower you to take full benefit of this fundamental rule: **"People love to buy from those whom they Know, Like and Trust"**. So remember to set up your profile in such a way that it helps people to KNOW you, LIKE you and TRUST you.

I know most direct sellers build their business alongside a job or some other profession. I also started the same way in 2007. So as I guide you on setting up your profile today, I have two objectives in mind for you:

1. Your profile shouldn't put your job or profession in jeopardy.
2. Your profile should help you in building your business by attracting and retaining the right people.

What you will learn today will help you meet both these objectives at the same time on the same profile.

With this fundamental clarity, let's discuss the different things on your profile one by one.

#1. Profile picture

Your profile picture is the first thing people notice when they come to your social media page. I recommend that you choose a solo photo of yours as your profile picture. A profile picture is not the place to show your recent trip, hobbies, passions, family, friends or get-togethers. It has to be you! You are the face of your account and that's what people want to see.

Choose a photo with a plain or minimal background. If you don't have such a photo right now, ask someone to click one for you. A studio photo is not mandatory but it must be a clearly visible close-up with good resolution. I recommend you keep the same picture or avatar across all different social media platforms. After uploading the photo, please don't forget to check how the photo is actually looking on your page. Zoom or crop it to give it the desired fit.

#2. Cover picture

A cover picture is the largest visual space you have on your page to show the world who you are and what you do. Some call it a banner image as well. Almost all major social media platforms have a cover picture option except Instagram, which instead has a unique feature called highlights. While you should not change your profile picture often, you can change your cover picture periodically.

Your cover picture is the place to declare your brand to the world and to let people instantly know what you do with one line or image. Every platform has different specifications, so design your cover picture as per those specifications. Use your cover picture to showcase what you do, your passion, your expertise or a compelling reason why should people follow you. It's actually a hook to attract people, to start a conversation and to keep them on your profile. A landscape image with or without a line works perfect as a cover image. You can use your own image or some other image or icon that depicts your brand value.

#3. Screen name or username

Every platform requires you to have a username or screen name that generally appears in all searches and shows on your profile along with your name. Select a good username that goes well with your work and is easy to remember for your audience. Don't pick up anything crazy to showcase your creativity. Go for something that you won't regret in a few months' or years' time when your brand will be bigger.

#4. About section or bio

Your bio or about section is the place on your social media profile where you write about your brand value and how you add value to people. It usually contains two fundamental pieces of information:

1. Who are you?
2. Why should someone follow you?

For the first one, describe in one or two lines what you do or what you believe in and how you are adding value to others.

The second one needs something more than just your city, profession, degrees, education etc. You need to give a compelling reason as to why others should follow you. We don't want the whole world to follow you but we definitely want your target audience to follow you, and this section is about presenting your work in a way that gives them a reason to follow you and stay connected with you.

All of us have a tendency to remember and associate with people who we like, who represent our values, who have similar interests and hobbies or who can be of some help in the future. So briefly mention whatever you are good at and whatever you want to promote here. But don't forget the golden rule that if your goal is to recruit people for your direct selling business, don't talk about direct selling in your bio. Almost every social media platform has a word limit for writing a bio; stay within that limit. And even if there isn't one, make sure you follow the SIP formula – Short, Interesting and Precise. Also don't forget to complete all fields, including your education and jobs, especially on LinkedIn.

Four expert tips for a great profile

1. Never forget that your social media profile is not for signing up or recruiting people but for initiating connection and conversation. You should propose your products or business opportunity only after doing proper prospecting. I will explain this more in the chapter on social media sales funnels.
2. Cross-promote your social media accounts by giving the links of your other social media accounts in every profile.

3. Complete all sections of your profile. Keep updating it regularly as things change in your personal and business life.
4. Periodically visit your profile using incognito mode to see how it would appear to your viewers.

So review your current profile today based on everything you have learned in this chapter and make the necessary changes. I wish you great connections.

> *"I follow three rules: Do the right thing, do the best you can, and always show people you care."*
>
> — Lou Holtz

REMEMBER AND SHARE

- Your profile is your first impression and people make a lot of judgments about you by looking at your profile. You should aim to set up your profile in such a way that people should feel like clicking and knowing more about you and later, becoming a friend or follower.
- You need to give a compelling reason in your bio or about section as to why should someone follow you.
- You should never put your company's name in your bio.
- Your profile is not for signing up or recruiting people but to initiate a connection and conversation.

KEY ACTIONS TO TAKE

- Review your profile on all your social media accounts and update the same immediately based on what you have learned in this chapter.

CHAPTER 6

How To Post Like a Pro

"You are responsible for everything you post and everything you post will be a reflection of you."

— GERMANY KENT

ONE ACTIVITY THAT YOU will be doing multiple times every day is posting on social media. This is going to be one of your key daily activities for many years to come and that's why we have dedicated this chapter exclusively to posting. This chapter is your complete guide to posting on social media. I have divided this chapter into two parts – first, we will discuss the 5 key components of posting and then I will share with you 13 expert guidelines that the world's best social media influencers and business builders are personally using. Let's begin with understanding the 5 key components of posting.

#1. Know your target audience

Many people think of social media as an ocean filled with lakhs of prospects swimming around and that you go there, cast your net and catch them. This approach is a total disaster for the simple reason that not everyone is right for you and you are not right for everyone. You are unique with your specific personality and specific message. Social media is a place to use your uniqueness to your advantage and that is what makes social media different from advertising.

Your uniqueness is your key to break through the clutter and attract people who resonate with your message and uniqueness. Trying to get anyone and everyone into your business is a total waste. You must identify your target audience because identifying your target market helps you recognize who the best prospects are, with whom you would like to spend time and build business.

> *"The most important thing to remember is you must know your audience."*
> — LEWIS HOWES

I have already shared with you the KLT rule of selling – *all things being equal, people prefer to do business with those whom they Know, Like and Trust.* So before they can like or trust you, you should clearly understand whose trust you are seeking. Audience analysis will help you with that. Once you have clearly defined your target audience then you should apply the KLT rule to every post. So whenever you post anything on social media, ask yourself these three questions:

1. Is this post or video going to increase the feeling in people that they KNOW me better?
2. Will this post or video increase the chances that they will LIKE me?
3. Is this post or video likely to increase their level of TRUST in me?

Don't share any post or video for which you don't get at least 2 "yes" answers out of 3.

#2. Captivating description or caption

A description is what you write below the post or video. You can decide the best description for your post based on your objective for that post. Ask yourself: what do you want to convey through that post, or what is your CTA (call to action) for that post? A post description should be designed to achieve your objective. Just in case you are not clear about what a CTA is, here is the simple definition – a CTA is what you want your audience to do after watching that video or post. If you have a clear CTA for the post, please include the same in your description, like "Follow me", "Share this post", "Take this action", "Call on this number", "Comment below" etc.

 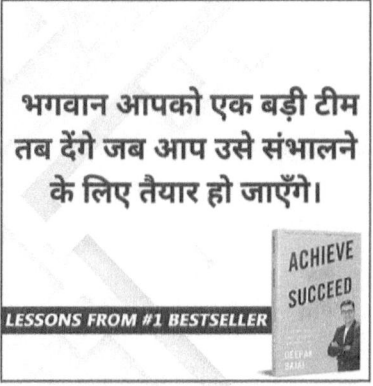

Start your description with a catchy headline. Many people decide to read or not to read the entire description after reading the headline and maybe 1 or 2 more sentences. So you'd better make it compelling. Keep your description precise. Don't write an essay. Write only whatever is necessary. Most of the platforms have a limit on the number of characters or words you can have in the description. Stick to that. Sometimes you can use attention-grabbing emojis to express your brand, personality or current mood but be smart about it, because overdoing it is not recommended.

Find and use relevant hashtags to a limited extent to multiply organic reach. Mentioning relevant accounts also helps increase your reach, but only mention accounts that are relevant or have some connection with that post. Overdoing it will look like spamming. Never just write one really long paragraph. Always divide it into shorter and relevant bits to ensure reader convenience.

Incorrect spelling and grammar don't give a good impression about you. If you are doubtful, write the description in Microsoft Word, Notes or any other app with a spelling and grammar checker. After that, simply copy the corrected text over into the description. Writing or speaking English doesn't give you any edge over using any other language. Grammatically correct Hindi is much better than broken or wrong English. Use the language that your target audience is most comfortable with. The best language to use is the language of your target audience.

A few good options to start your description with (headlines):

- How to _____
- Quick guide for _____
- A complete guide to _____
- Questions you should ask before _____
- Rules for _____
- Essential steps to _____
- Most popular ways to _____
- Tips for busy _____
- Tactics to _____
- What no one tells you about _____

These are a few classic opening lines that have been giving excellent results for thousands of my course participants and myself. You can experiment with these and a few more of your own to select the ones that work the best with your audience.

#3. Relevant hashtags

Hashtags are the vehicles that take your content to newer audiences who were not following you already. Hashtags also mean taking part in the conversation already happening on social media. They always start with a # (hash) symbol but they won't work if you use spaces, punctuation or symbols. Make sure that the hashtags that you are using are relevant to your post. Just using any hashtag for the sake of using it is a total waste. It makes your post look like spam. When you are posting about a cooking video, don't use hashtags for travel, entrepreneurship, business etc.

Make sure your accounts are public, otherwise your hashtagged content will not reach out to non-followers. Don't string too many words together. The best hashtags tend to be relatively short and easy to remember. Also limit the number of hashtags you use. More isn't always better; rather, it actually looks spammy. There is no set rule about how many hashtags are good for a post. You can check the same online from reliable influencers or experiment with different numbers of them on your posts.

I can tell you from experience that you should prepare a collection of hashtags and keep it handy. You can quickly select from that list while posting. It will save you a lot of time and energy. You can find the top and trending hashtags for your brand or industry from a plethora of websites. Doing this research once in a while is also rewarding.

#4. DRPF – daily recommended posting frequency

It needs guts to address something as controversial as daily recommended posting frequency for social media platforms because these recommendations keep changing like the phases of the moon. So many gurus, experts and influencers keep giving new information about this every other day, but you can search for the latest recommendations whenever you want. But I suggest that you should experiment with a different number of posts at different timings of the day to find out what gets the best engagement with your audience and go for the same. Whatever frequency you decide on, the rule of thumb is to make sure that you are seen and you are in front of your followers at least once every day.

#5. Social media calendar

Illustration 5

A social media calendar is an advance plan for your posts for the entire one or two upcoming weeks. Most of you have multiple tasks to complete during the day and it is not humanly possible to post the best-quality content at the right time every single day. That's where a social media calendar comes in handy. Personally, I have seen that a social media calendar is one of the best ways to ensure the quality and consistency of your posting. It also helps you plan ahead for upcoming festivals or special days. You can set aside 2-4 hours per week to prepare posts for the next whole week.

Start creating your social media calendar on Google Sheets or MS Excel with a few key columns, like the platform, date, time, description, hashtags, visual elements, link to assets, status (in progress/scheduled/published) etc. A lot of mobile apps and software are also available but honestly, you don't need them because learning them would be another subject in itself.

Posting strategies of the world's best influencers

After closely observing and interviewing some of the best social media influencers/accounts for a long period of time, I have found out some of the best practices for posting on social media. I have personally used them and so have thousands of my course participants. I am sharing the best ones with you here:

#1. 3 Cs of posting

Remember these 3 Cs and your post will reach out to the maximum people and have maximum impact.

4. **Cutting through** – Your post designs should be so attractive that they cut through the clutter of social media and catch the attention of your target audience instantly.
5. **Consistency** – Post every single day.
6. **Congruency** – You should post content strictly around your core brand value and not on any random topic. Don't post a motivational video today morning, a cooking recipe in the evening and relationship suggestions the next day. Every post should strengthen your brand value and establish

your authority in your core area. You will know your brand is established when you are the first person people contact whenever they need any information related to your area.

#2. You will win the game by being one among them

> *"Don't use social media to impress people,
> use it to impact people."*
> — DAVE WILLIS

When it comes to connecting with people on social media, you should appear accessible and similar to them. If you want to convince them with the idea that anyone can do what you do, then you need to present yourself as one among them. It is smarter to present yourself as a human, not a superhuman. Your real goal is to let people say, *"If this person can do it, then so can I."*

If you think the goal is to impress people, you have failed before you have even started. So let it be real. It is also fine to share your struggles and challenges as long as you don't dwell too much on self-pity. Let your followers be a part of your journey as you overcome your challenges.

#3. Model others, but don't copy

It's always good to learn from influencers and leaders, but never copy anyone. Everyone has different goals and personalities and are at different stages in their career. If you love something that is in alignment with your core brand value, you can share it and give credit to the original creator. But your followers are on your page for you. So be yourself and follow your own style.

#4. Value posts work the best to build your credibility

Every person on social media, including you and me, asks this question before reading any post or before following anyone: **WIIFM (what's in it for me?)**. Value posts are the answer to this question. Why should people follow you? People should follow you because whatever you are sharing is of interest or value to them. Principally, all those posts that provide solutions to the problems of your followers or inspire or empower them are called value posts. Value posts are extremely important as they get your target audience to follow you and stick with you. Value posts get you people, make people stick, engage and wait for your next posts, motivate them to keep visiting your page and finally one day will make them show interest and buy your product or accept your business proposal.

Any post can be called a value post only when it fulfills these five criteria:

1. Delivering content that is of value to your target audience with no expectations of immediate return.
2. No links embedded in the post or description.
3. No mention of your company or products.
4. No mention of your profession or opportunity.
5. No sales hype lines like "No competition", "New billion-dollar opportunity", "Super easy", "Now or never offer" etc.

Become a master of creating value posts. 70-90% of your content should be value posts.

#5. Don't keep checking for likes or comments every half an hour

Share your post and get busy with your regular work. Don't keep checking for likes or comments every time you pick up your phone. Stick to your timings or check the performance of previous posts while uploading the next post.

#6. Videos are getting better engagement than posts

As of my writing of this book, video posts are getting many times more engagement than image posts and it seems this trend is going to stay for some more time in the near future. So it is recommended to share more video content on your social media accounts.

#7. Keep it entertaining

Variety adds spice to your social media profile. However good your content is, repetitive content gets boring after a certain period. So keep your audience engaged and entertained with variety. Find new, creative ways of sharing the same content.

"There is no 'one-size-fits-all' way to build an audience."
— John Stuart Mill

#8. Keep experimenting

Social media is truly dynamic and trends change here faster than you or I could possibly imagine. In fact, this dynamism is one of the key drivers for the massive rise of social media. My rule of thumb for getting good results from social media: *assume less, experiment more.* Keep trying new things every now and then, and as you try new things, do what my coach always tells me: *"Do more of what is working and do less of what is not working."*

#9. Always look at the long term

Value-adding content shared consistently will never go unrewarded. You never know what post will reach where or which one will give you the breakthrough you always wanted. So have patience and always look at the long term.

#10. The 4G1A rule of social media

The top income earners always work with the 4G1A rule of social media – give, give, give, give and ask. You need to give value at least 4 times before you earn the privilege of asking anything from your audience. This rule is an indicator of the underlying philosophy of social media – you need to give 4 times more value than what you expect your audience to give you. Personally, we follow the 10G1A rule in our organization. Any time we deliver an online course or live event, we always work with the philosophy that we must give 10 times more value to our participants than what they have paid for.

#11. Never let the fear of making mistakes stop you from posting

Social media is not a classroom skill; it's a 'doing' skill and the best way to learn it is by practicing what you learn. That's why I have given tasks at the end of every chapter. Why have people across the globe been getting incredible results from each of my online courses? The reason is my unique teaching methodology that focuses on daily activities and tasks. That's how you actually master any skill. So if you really want to master social media, just go out and do it. Make mistakes, learn from them and keep getting better.

Don't let this fear of making mistakes paralyze you from posting. Take action right now with whatever you know and whatever resources you have. As you reach the next milestone, the universe will show you the way forward.

#12. Adaptability

Technology, algorithms and people's habits will continue to change so we entrepreneurs will also have to change and adapt. At one point of time, photos were doing great on social media, then came infographics; now it's videos and nobody knows what the next big thing will be. So be open, be flexible and be adaptable.

#13. Do not oversell your business on your page

Don't be insensitive to your followers and never forget that a user can block you in one second. Your followers should feel that they are following a human being they can relate to and not another salesperson. Yes, I know, selling is important and you have business objectives for operating your social media account. But your social media page is not the place for selling. You can share your product or business benefits once in a while but do it like a consultant and not a salesperson.

These expert strategies have already given incredible results to thousands of people. Why not you? Why not now?

If you have been spamming your account with a lot of company or product posts in the past, or if you have made posts that you now think were not good for your brand and reputation, you can delete some content that you posted in the last one or two weeks. Alternatively, you can just forget about what you have posted in the past and start posting the right things from today. People have a short memory. They will forget the past sooner than you will.

> *"Remember during your interactions that social media was made for people, not businesses."*
>
> — JAY BAER

REMEMBER AND SHARE

- The KLT rule of selling – all things being equal, people prefer to do business with those whom they Know, Like and Trust.
- Hashtags are the vehicles that take your content to newer audiences who were not your followers. Use short and relevant hashtags with you posts.
- Prepare and schedule your posts at least one week in advance with a social media calendar.
- The 3 Cs of Posting – Cutting through, Consistency and Congruency.
- Your goal is not to impress people on social media but to look accessible and be one among them.
- Don't put your products, income statements or business event invitations on your profile.
- The 4G1A rule of social media – Give, Give, Give, Give and Ask.
- Keep changing and adapting to the changes in technology, algorithms and people's habits.

KEY ACTIONS TO TAKE

- Make your social media calendar.
- Build your collection of hashtags for using in your posts.
- List down the 3 best ideas from this chapter that you will always use while posting.
- Share the key learnings from this chapter with your team.

CHAPTER 7

The 11-Point System for Creating Never-Ending Content

"Content isn't king, it's the kingdom."
— LEE ODDEN

POSTING IS GOOD, PHOTOS are fun and videos are still manageable but when it comes to writing content, many people are scared to death. This chapter aims to simplify content creation and content management in such a way that you are able to joyfully create a never-ending supply of impactful and engaging content day after day, month after month and year after year.

Anything that you post on any of your social media platforms is content. All the photos, infographics, videos, podcasts or written articles are different forms of content. I consider any content to be good only if it does one of these two:

1. Gives solutions that help solve some of the problems of your audience
2. Provides insights that can inspire or empower them to reach their goals faster

The better the solutions and insights you provide with your content, the higher the level of engagement and loyalty from your audience will be. Content is what brings people to your page and, most importantly, keeps people on your page. You may get people to visit your page through attractive designs or paid digital marketing efforts, but good-quality and value-adding content is absolutely essential to retain your friends and followers. It is also the right content that gets you all the likes, comments, shares and saves. Now let's understand 11 key components that you need to master for creating great content.

#1. Relevance and utility of the content

Do you know why all my books rose to #1 bestseller status within a few hours of their launch? Why my YouTube channel is considered as the most reliable and sought-after free training academy by direct sellers from 100-plus countries? Why my online courses are the #1 choice for direct sellers in every company across the globe? If your answer is 'content', you are absolutely right. But what makes our content special is the utility and relevance of the content. We never create anything just for the sake of posting it; we make sure that every word we write is useful for our audience.

The best of content is totally wasted if it doesn't help your audience. Content is not about you; it's about your audience. Your content has to give answers, solutions and value to your target audience.

Find out exactly what your audience is looking for. What are their challenges and aspirations? Then craft your content to serve them and help them. Speak their language. Be on their side and create something that is useful to your audience. There is only one real test of good content and that is the benefit it delivers to the audience.

> *"When we create something, we think, 'Will our customers thank us for this?'"*
>
> — Ann Handley

#2. Compelling and shareable content

As per the Oxford Dictionary, something 'compelling' is something that forces or persuades you to believe something and take action. So aim to create content that is compelling. Ask yourself these two questions before you post your content:

1. What do you want your audience to do or think as a result of watching this content?
2. Will this content actually make them do the same?

Post the content only if you get a 'yes' for the second question. Here's one of the tests to check if you are making the right kind of content: how many shares are you getting for your content? Sharing is the real test of engagement. Likes are ok but when your audience is sharing your content, that is when you know that your content is connecting with and serving your audience.

#3. The latest content

Do you know why so many college graduates and post-graduates struggle to get a job after they finish their degree? The biggest reason is that the skills that they learned in their college had become outdated before they even graduated. You cannot solve today's problems with the knowledge and tools of yesterday. Things are changing faster than you can possibly imagine. In 2021, people don't need solutions that worked in the 1990s or 2000s. So your content has to remain current and updated. You should provide real-time solutions for current problems.

Why are a majority of direct sellers struggling today? Most of them are working with tools that their upline's upline's upline learned 15 years ago. Those skills and tools are not wrong, but they fail to give results today because people have changed. The habits, behavior and lifestyle of people have totally changed and if you want to build a business today, you need to work with today's mindset, skillset and toolset. So give your audience the content that genuinely addresses their ongoing challenges.

#4. Content creation ideas

The kind of content you will create depends on your own expertise and the brand you are trying to build, but here are some general ideas and topics with which you can create never-ending content:

- Attention-grabbing and inspirational quotes
- Tips and tricks
- How-to content
- Personalized content – like BTS (behind the scenes) photos, a sneak peek at your favorites, before and afters, origin story, a picture of the book you're reading, bucket list etc.
- Industry facts, statistics or articles
- Flat lay pictures
- Events or festivals
- Ask different kinds of questions like "Truth or myth", "Would you rather...", polls or fill in the blanks, ask for predictions or simply answer questions that people ask you
- Testimonials or reviews
- Current events or what's trending

Keep changing your content type to give a variety to and surprise your audience.

#5. Content bank

Building a content bank is one of my all-time favorite strategies that has helped me provide the best-quality content to my followers regularly. A content bank is a pool of content that you have prepared with the intention of posting it in the future. It's a collection of ready-to-post content that you will post on one or more platforms in the days or weeks to come.

A content bank not only helps you in producing good-quality content but also helps in maintaining consistency of posting. It eliminates the last-minute stress of brainstorming or designing creative content. Get started with your content bank by making a simple content management system on your mobile phone or laptop with folders like 'Used', 'Next Week', 'Bank' etc.

#6. A stock of your own photos

Another thing you will need often for posting on different social media accounts is your own photos. So always keep your photo folder handy and keep saving your best photos there. Get into the habit of taking good pictures of yourself wherever you go. You can get some good studio photos or ask some of your friends to click some good pictures for you.

Keep 2-3 photos with different backgrounds. Keep a few formal and casual photos that you can use regularly. Get the backgrounds removed for a few photos so that they can be fitted on different backgrounds as well.

#7. Content sources

Since you are creating content related to your own brand values, you can create a lot of content by yourself with your existing knowledge and experience. But at the same time, you can get excellent quality content through some of these resources:

- Google
- YouTube
- Books
- Magazines
- Your own notes
- Training programs
- Events
- Leading social media influencers
- Industry leaders in your domain

Whenever you are taking content from somewhere, don't forget to give them due credit. Don't post someone else's content under your own name. When you give credit to others, it speaks well about your character and attitude. You can also do keyword and topic research to find out what is trending. That will keep your content fresh and relevant.

> *"Content precedes design. Design in the absence of content is not design, it's decoration."*
> — JEFFREY ZEIDMAN

#8. Curate content

While you can create your own original content, you can also use content created by others in your domain to share on your platforms. That kind of content is called curated content. You can forward or share the content of others as it is by giving them due credit, or use some of it as part of your content.

A combination of original and curated content keeps your content calendar full and provides a variety of complete knowledge to your audience. Curating is different from copying. Never copy content from others. You actually don't need to. How long will you copy for and who all will you copy from? It's a long-term game. Most of your followers will also be following industry leaders and they will instantly make out that you are putting someone else's content under your name and that will spoil your reputation.

#9. Content redistribution

Content redistribution simply means using one form of content to create multiple forms of content. This is an excellent strategy that will save you a lot of time and effort. Create one piece of content and then edit it to make content in different formats. For example, let's say you shot a video for YouTube. Now you can make so many different forms of content from this single piece of YouTube content – IGTV videos, Facebook or Instagram videos, LinkedIn videos, posts, carousels, blog posts, podcasts, reels, stories etc. As you begin this journey, you will gradually become a master at this.

#10. Batch creation

This is another one of my favorites that I personally use quite often and it saves me lot of time and energy. I have understood from my own experience that content creation needs a different mental state than working in an office or field. So I highly recommend that whenever you are in a creative state, you should make several pieces of content together at the same time. I always prepare 2-4 video scripts in advance and then shoot them all in one batch.

Batch creation is particularly good for new creators and for those who are doing multiple things other than just creating content. Use a content bank, a social media calendar and batch creation of content for more efficient content creation and posting.

#11. Respect your audience

I am very emotional about this particular subject. When people are giving you their time and attention, it's your moral responsibility to deliver your best. You must give more than 100% of your efforts and commitment. I have seen some people who are just in a race to create non-stop content. I don't have any problems with this strategy as long as you deliver relevant and useful content. But I highly recommend that you respect your audience, and one of the ways you can do that is by providing them with your best content.

Always work with the genuine intention to add value to your followers. It works like magic, and wherever I have reached today is because of this one single philosophy that I personally follow and everyone in my organization also follows – we must give 10 times more value to our clients than the price we charge for any of our products. We must wow our customers with 10 times more value than they expect.

Every person who registers for our online programs gets reminder calls or notifications from our team to check if they have been watching the program and to see how their progress has been. We provide 24/7 support through our private mentorship groups so that people don't just get a course but also achieve the results that they need the most. We believe selling an event ticket or an online program is not the end of the process; it's actually the beginning of our partnership. It costs us quite a lot to offer this kind of service but the smiles on the faces of our customers and the results they get with this system give us the greatest joy and convert our customers into raving fans. When you care for your people, they care for you and your business.

In summary, I would like to remind you that you are unique and that this is your superpower. There will be times when you may doubt yourself, your content or the way you are managing your social media, or fear that the content that you are creating has already been created by many different people and so on. Please remember this is natural and happens with everyone. But the world needs to hear your voice and your unique message. Don't quit and just continue with the process.

> *"Actually talk to your customers. Use the language that they use. Talk about the things they talk about. Never feed salad to a lion."*
>
> — JAY ACUNZO

REMEMBER AND SHARE

- Good content should provide either of these two to your audience – solutions to their problems or insights to help them reach their goals faster.
- It's not about being right but about the relevance and utility of your content.
- A content bank, content redistribution and batch creation are critical for consistent posting.
- Every time you create new content, ask yourself: what do you want your audience to do or think as a result of watching this content?
- A combination of original and curated content keeps your content calendar full and gives a variety of complete knowledge to your audience.
- Respect your audience. When people are giving you their time and attention, it's your moral responsibility to deliver your best. Wow your audience with your work.

KEY ACTIONS TO TAKE

- Identify the areas you need to work on for effective content creation.
- Make your own content creation strategy based on what you have learned in today's lesson.

CHAPTER 8

How To Maximize Your Impact and Gain New Followers Organically

"Social media is not about the exploitation of technology but service to community."

— SIMON MAINWARING

ONCE YOUR PROFILE IS set, you've started creating valuable content and you've started posting consistently, the next goal should be to multiply your effectiveness and results. You need to find ways to maximize the reach of your content, the organic growth of your followers and the impact of your work because that is the route to getting the desired results from your social media efforts. This chapter will give you strategies and insights to maximize your impact and gain new followers organically without spending money on paid promotions or complicated digital marketing. Let's understand the 11 result maximizers now.

Result Maximizer #1
Never assume; always ask

Many people make the mistake of assuming that they know their audience too well and keep pushing boring and useless content in the hope that it will bring results someday. Ironically, that day never comes. So it is always smarter to keep asking your audience exactly what they want. Ask how you can serve them better and give them more value. And when I tell you to ask your audience, I definitely don't expect you to put up a post asking them.

Being in touch with your audience, reading their comments, being connected to ongoing industry trends, live sessions, question and answer sessions etc. are some of the different ways to know exactly what your audience needs. Interestingly, sometimes what your followers need is much easier to provide than what you have been struggling to give them. If you keep asking them, it can save you many years of hard work and will also keep your content relevant and useful.

Result Maximizer #2
Use new and different features

All good social media platforms are constantly innovating and working round the clock to add new features so that they can keep their users hooked to their platform. User experience and people retention is the ultimate goal for every social media platform because that is their only way to survive and thrive. But new features are useless if a big chunk of their audience doesn't use them. So every time they launch any new feature, social media platforms strive to make that new feature popular faster. They do this by aggressively promoting all the content that uses those new features, especially in the first few weeks of the launch.

So if you can spot any new feature on a social media platform and start using it while creating your content, the social media platform will automatically take your content to people who have not already been following you. Be smart and keep your eyes and ears open for new features. If you are following influencers in your domain, you will easily be able to spot such new features by looking at their content. So spot the trends and be the first mover whenever you can.

> "The social media landscape changes incredibly fast, so you have to be open-minded and nimble to keep up with it."
> — Alexis Ohanian

Result Maximizer #3
Nobody wants to see direct selling on your page

Let's face it – nobody wants to see network marketing or direct selling posts or be friends with someone who is always talking about his products and his company, asking you to join him etc. So remember to keep your social media page personal. Don't make it a business-broadcasting channel.

Your content's main purpose is to give people a reason to come to your page, stay with it, fall in love with it, engage with it and gradually build a connection with you and build a relationship. This is the fundamental principle that you should never break. If you are confident that your opportunity really is wonderful, why do you want to offer it to each and every person without even checking if they are suitable for it or not? Why are you desperate to talk about business on first sight? This is the sign of an amateur. Master the entire business-building process for online businesses and use social media only for what it is meant for.

Result Maximizer #4
Focus on activity and not results

As you have reached this point in this book, I am sure you are not one of those people who start posting and expect new recruits by the 3rd post itself. Please understand this is one key reason why many people who start social media with great enthusiasm quit within the first few weeks of starting. Whenever you start building your social media page, your first task is to build a pipeline – a pipeline that you will start filling with strangers who will turn into familiar acquaintances and eventually friends. You achieve this by providing consistent value throughout the process of nurturing the relationship.

So whenever you start your serious social media efforts, start with a commitment for consistent daily activity. Consider whatever results you get in the first few months as a stipend. The real magic will unfold once you have established a big base of connections in different stages of conversation. If you have been following my work, I call this activity developing your prospecting pool. After training more than 10 lakh direct sellers in the past 14 years, I can assure you that any direct seller who understands the concept of and builds a prospecting pool will never quit the business and will be able to build a big direct selling business. Please understand I am not against results; I always believe you should be a result-driven person. But I have realized that if you focus on results, you will never get results, whereas if you focus on daily actions, results are automatic. So keep results in mind but stay focused on daily activities.

> *"Ordinary people with extraordinary focus can create extraordinary achievements."*
>
> — DEEPAK BAJAJ

Result Maximizer #5
The world doesn't need one more guru

I have heard many people use the phrase *"fake it till you make it"*, and I am sure some people take it seriously and fake things one after the other. Fake pens, fake watches, fake income, fake lifestyle, fake followers, fake views, fake happiness etc. But I am yet to meet any such fake person who has achieved anything in reality. My question is, why fake it? Why pretend to be something you are not?

I have seen people who call themselves wealth coaches but have been living on a zero balance account, worried about how to pay next month's rent. I know people who have not achieved anything in life, but they claim themselves to be coaches who will create millionaires. Somehow, people are living with the misconception that claiming to be a guru or an expert will work and be a shortcut to success. But it doesn't work like that. I highly recommend you never pretend to be a guru or an authority. How long will you fake it? I have been telling you repeatedly that building your brand is a long-term strategy. You can fake it for a day or two, maybe a week, but you cannot fake it every day for so many months. This pressure to maintain your false identity will take up so much of your time, energy and mental space that you will not be left with any time or energy to actually work on your dreams.

Rather than pretending to be more than you are, why not just take people on your journey with you – from wherever you are to wherever you reach? That's the kind of person other people want to follow and be around. If you can talk about the things you have learned, even if you only learned them yesterday – things that will help make others' lives better – they won't care when you learned it or how much money you are worth. They will appreciate your efforts in helping them. I believe presenting yourself exactly as you are is the only sustainable model to follow. A lot of people keep suggesting tricks to me for gaining a few thousand more followers, but I have never done anything that is against my ethics and values. You will see a lot of YouTubers who use clickbait thumbnails, where the title on the thumbnail has no connection with the actual content of the video. People may click that thumbnail, but won't they feel cheated after watching the video? In the race to build a big direct selling business or a big social media account, never get into doing things that are not ethical.

Some direct sellers feel they will be able to do big business if they can show big achievements. I don't know if people decide to start with you by looking at your car or house, because I have done personal sponsoring both with an Alto car and a Mercedes-Benz. I have done prospecting and plan presentations with a 3 BHK rented house as well as a 10,000 sq. ft villa. I have not found any differences in my results because of the type of the car or size of the house. I have seen people with 10 gold rings on all their fingers and so many gold chains around their neck that their neck isn't even visible. I don't have any judgment for such leaders, but I could build a much bigger business, and faster, without a single ring or necklace.

If you have genuine achievements and you want to show them, then please do so – it's purely your personal decision – but I am strictly against making fake claims. Never claim anything that you have not earned or do not own. Some people fake it because they feel no one will notice their false claims on social media and others are worried that they cannot attract good people if they don't show off fancy things. Whatever your reason is for making fake claims, let me tell you one thing – if dishonesty is the foundation of your business, your business will never take off. If any relationship begins with a lie, I don't think it will have a very long life.

So here are some of my recommendations in this regard:

- Don't pose before someone else's car or mansion and say it's yours.
- Never lie about income.
- Never promote your one-time cheque as your monthly income.
- Don't lie about your rank, level or team size.

Never make fake income claims because sooner or later, the internet will expose you. Even if some people join you after seeing such claims, how will you face them when they are a part of your team? You are into a business, not into lotteries or gambling. Businesses take time. Everyone doesn't succeed. It's ok. People are mature and they understand these facts. Your lies cannot pull them to you. Never exaggerate. Have trust in yourself and build a business with confidence and posture.

Instead of spending money on buying fake things, invest that money in a good training or coaching program for your growth and development. You and your business are one and the same in network marketing so as you grow, your business will grow with you.

Result Maximizer #6
Meaningful collaborations

Collaborations have proved to be a great way to multiply your reach. Collaborations with other social media creators and thought leaders in your domain are a wonderful way to grow your influence and to serve your community. Collaboration, as the name suggests, simply means working together. Seek out creators in your domain whose working philosophy matches with yours and explore possible ways of working together – live sessions on each others' pages, doing an event together, doing some giveaways together or simply promoting each other's work. Just like with everything else, you can think of new, creative ideas for collaborations that suit you and your followers.

Approach other thought leaders in your industry and build connections with them – like their pages, comment regularly and follow their work. Compliment them. Be their best friend or follower and then ask for a suitable collaboration. If you cannot interview them, begin by sharing their work on your pages and as you do it consistently, they will start to notice. I have close to 10 lakh followers on different social media platforms but I know who my best followers are, who the first ones to like or comment are and who are with me on my mission. So be persistent and consistent – they may not say yes immediately but it will definitely work out in some way or the other.

I have simplified the process of asking for the right collaborations in an easy-to-remember formula that I call the 3 Cs to collaborate:

1. Compliment
2. Connect
3. Collaborate

Result Maximizer #7
Expect haters and negative comments

> *"You don't get to a million friends without creating a few enemies."*
> — DEEPAK BAJAJ

If you have the desire that everyone on social media should love you, admire you and understand your good work, then please don't even start. Wishing to not have haters or doubters is a stupid endeavor. Do you really want to know about a guaranteed way to not have critics and haters? Just don't do anything and live a life of anonymity. Just be a mute spectator and another face in the crowd. That is the only way to not have critics. But if you have any desire to make a big impact and build a business that you will be proud of, you will have to face haters and doubters. If you expect your social media account to reach out to lakhs of people and impact many lives, then haters and doubters are complementary. They will come along as part of the package.

But if you keep worrying about them, you will not have time to do the things that will fulfill your dreams. Also, you will miss out on many people who you could have impacted with the same energy and time that you wasted on haters. Remember, haters are normal; not having haters is a problem.

However good your work may be, expect some bad comments. You may feel upset and heartbroken at times. You will have an internal dialogue where you will sometimes doubt yourself and your work and you may even get into a negative spiral. I totally understand this because I have also gone through this many times. It's tough to accept negative comments, particularly when you are doing everything genuinely well. Just remember and respect the fact that people are different and you just cannot please everyone. The comments people write on social media don't show who you are, but they reflect who the authors are.

Take my own case, for example. I have written two books before the one you are reading right now. It took me more than one year of dedicated daily efforts to write 1,70,000-plus words of incredible, value-adding content in those two books. My books are generally available for Rs. 140-250 each if you buy an original copy and Rs. 50 for the pirated version. By the way, I have the designation of being one of the most pirated authors in my category.

As of writing of this book, there are more than 370 videos on my YouTube channel with an average duration of 10 minutes each. Each video is kind of a mini-course loaded with cutting-edge knowledge, skills and tools. I don't give motivational stories in my videos, but I give real tools that anyone can instantly apply and get results. If someone listens to them seriously for 8-10 hours a day and takes notes, it may take 10-15 days to really absorb that content. Conceptualizing, shooting, editing and posting one such video takes 2-4 days. That makes it 800-1,000 days. Practically 2-3 years of man-hours have been invested into producing this absolutely free, value-adding content. If you assume editing fees of only Rs. 5,000 per video, it will be Rs. 18.5 lakh. Add to this my own time and experience – that is priceless. I care for my audience so much that I have not even monetized my YouTube channel so that my viewers get the best possible experience.

I have made all of this available to people for free but then there are also people who don't even blink before writing a negative comment. Initially I used to ask myself, "What could I do about this?" But now I have understood – I cannot convince everyone. Whatever I may say, people will take it with their own understanding, beliefs and opinions.

Some negative comments are natural. Don't worry. The best response is to ignore them. But if something is worth fighting for, fight and take a stand gracefully. How you answer a negative comment or handle criticism is a true mark of your leadership and I know you will do so gracefully.

> *"The power of social media is when it is built on top of real activity."*
>
> — DAVID BATSTONE

Result Maximizer #8
Never criticize other companies

If some direct selling company closes down or there is some negative news about a company, it's not time for you to celebrate and spread the news. Talking negatively about other companies will never get you any good results. It tarnishes the whole profession. Share all the good you want to share about your company without saying anything bad about any other company.

Result Maximizer #9
Never put down jobs or other professions

You don't need to put somebody down to show that you are better. Putting down jobs or demeaning college degrees or other professions reflects badly on you. And as a matter of fact, it's not even true. People are thriving in their jobs and professions. There are a countless number of employees and professionals who are earning well and have an excellent social status. Direct selling is not a lottery or jackpot. It's a profession or business like any other and your task is to highlight how it can help your prospects in fulfilling their dreams or solving some of their problems.

Never say, "You are part of the problem", "You are in a rat race" etc. You have no right to judge people. Everyone has their own unique dreams and ways of accomplishing those dreams. Their life is their choice and not yours. You can encourage people to strive for more, but never put down whatever they are doing. You can never win them over like this; rather, such behavior will close doors for the future. Make them product customers if not distributors. Who knows? They could be among some of the biggest business builders in your organization in the future.

Result Maximizer #10
Spamming is intolerable

We all have been taught good manners while dealing with people and the expected behavior for when we are in public. Likewise, for social media, we need to understand and follow some good manners and conduct. A few activities that are not expected from good people on social media and are considered spamming are given below. You must refrain from indulging in the same.

- Never post your offers in the comments section of somebody else's posts. It looks horrible. It speaks badly about you and your company. It's clearly a signal of your frustration and desperation and you will get only one result from this – people will hate you.
- Never engage in unsolicited tagging – don't tag others without their permission. Also, don't tag people in posts that are not related to them. Tagging once in a while is still acceptable, but don't tag people frequently.
- Even if you disagree with some point, don't use bad words or forbidden words in a comments section. It speaks more about you than about the other person.
- Never hijack your friends' friends. Don't start mass messaging your friends' friends.

Just imagine what all this would do to your reputation or brand image. Who would respond to or love to connect with a person who behaves like this? It would ultimately kill your reputation and business.

Result Maximizer #11
Never stop learning

> *"Growth is life. The day you stop learning, you stop growing; the day you stop growing, you are dead."*
> — Deepak Bajaj

I strongly believe that your current level of income and success is a reflection of your current level of knowledge, mindset and skills. If you want to multiply the level of your success, income or lifestyle, you need to elevate your mindset, skillset and toolset. Ever-evolving technology, transparency, easily accessible information and growing aspirations have dramatically changed the ways of working in the last few years. The lifestyle, culture and behavior of people have been changing rapidly. Any person or business that is not able to keep pace with this change will soon be out of the business. So make constant learning your topmost priority.

Some people feel practice will make them perfect. Practice can make you good at doing what you have been doing, but it doesn't make you better. For better results, you need to practice better things. I am surprised to see thousands of direct sellers at the same income today where they have been 10 years ago. Every year, they are becoming experts at staying the same. Sad. Really sad. They are doing the same things again and again and hence their results are also the same. Every year, they have been performing worse and earning less.

Social media is dynamic. The rules of entrepreneurship are changing by the second. Sometimes, one new idea learned in any online course or live event can totally change your game. Keep learning new things and continue upgrading your mindset, skillset and toolset. Always remember that all the time and effort that you will be putting into upscaling your social media game will be an investment in a bright, secure, free and abundant future. Your current goal is to get a few new members that can help you with one or two of your struggling teams, or who can get you some extra volume for qualifying your targets, but the real benefit of mastering social media will be revealed in a few months or years.

Last month, I was doing one high-performance coaching session with a girl from Surat. She is just 22 years old and running the first business of her life. She started her direct selling business with a stranger from Punjab and has built a team of more than 220 associates during a few months of lockdown. But the most interesting thing in her success story is the fact that she has never met her upline face-to-face, nor has she ever met any one of her 220 teammates. She started the business online through social media and built her entire team online using social media and online tools. She has already started earning an income of more than Rs. 1 lakh per month. Thousands of participants from my online course, *Social Media and Online Business Mastery*, have reported similar transformational success stories. Social media and online business-building tools have given a new direction and momentum to thousands of direct sellers around the world. But can you guess what is common among all these success stories? They have made constant learning and growth their #1 priority. To grow faster than the rest, you must continue learning and growing faster than everybody else.

It's not about first-mover advantage any more now; it's entirely about fast-mover advantage. These 11 result multipliers have the potential to make you a super-fast achiever. Just get to action and start implementing them today. I know you are a fast mover. Make it happen.

> *"Each person has the potential of making a positive impact on the world. It all depends on what you do with what you have."*
>
> — GARY CHAPMAN

REMEMBER AND SHARE

- Your personal page has to be yours and not about your company, product or business.
- Don't pretend to be a guru and never fake your income or achievements.
- Promote, share and bring value to other people or organizations in the same domain as yours. When you do good things, better things will come your way.
- Never criticize other companies and never put down jobs or other professions.
- As you grow, so will the number of your haters and doubters. Never waste your energy on them. Keep building your dream.
- Network marketing and social media are dynamic. Keep upgrading your mindset, skillset and toolset.

KEY ACTIONS TO TAKE

- Write down 3 key strategies from this chapter that you will start implementing immediately to multiply your influence on social media.
- Analyze 5 good social media accounts in the same domain as yours and find out what are they doing right.

CHAPTER 9

Choosing the Right Social Media Platform for You

"Social tools are not just about giving people a voice, but giving them a way to collaborate, contribute and connect."

— John Stepper

ONE OF THE KEY determinants of your success on social media is the platform on which you are operating. It's not that any platform is good or bad, it's about finding the platform that you love working with and that gives you the maximum return on the time you invest. You need to find the best fit for yourself and this chapter will empower you to smartly make this choice by giving you a few insights and concepts. Here are three key things you should consider while choosing the best platform for you:

1. Which platform is your target audience using the most?
2. What is your preferred form of content?
3. Where do you get the maximum traction for your content?

While you can build your brand on multiple platforms, you should invest your maximum time on the platform that has the type of people you are most trying to attract. So identify 2-3 social media platforms that serve you the best and start building your brand there. One of the reasons why

I am recommending 2-3 platforms is because of the dynamic nature of social media platforms. The platform that is giving you excellent results today may change at any time. So when you are building 2-3 platforms together, it gives you the leverage plus the flexibility to keep moving among platforms.

Also, building any social media account requires a lot of time and effort. Working on more than 3 channels will not leave you with any time left to build a business and manage other things in life. If you work on more than 3 channels, it will also dissipate your influence because as the engagement, number of followers and content base of your channel grow, so does your credibility and the likelihood of new prospects to start following you. As an audience starts interacting with your content, social media algorithms start supporting you by spreading your content to new audiences and this puts you on a growth trajectory. As new platforms are being launched every day, there will always be this temptation to start building your account there but trust me, even if you work 24 hours a day on social media, there will still be platforms that you would not be able to cover.

I am sure you will have seen some direct sellers who continue hopping from one direct selling company to another in the hope of striking a jackpot and getting some quick success. Such direct selling junkies never succeed, and I know some of them who have been repeating this process for more than a decade now and have still not found the perfect company. Rather, people have started asking them: *"What is the next big thing you have got this time?"* I always recommend that direct sellers don't look for the best company; instead, look for the right company who is following all government guidelines and whose products you believe in. Once you have identified the right company and the right upline, then you should devote all your focus and efforts towards building your team and multiplying business volume. If you want help in selecting the right direct selling company, you can find a comprehensive chapter on this in both my books – *Achieve More, Succeed Faster* and *Be a Network Marketing Millionaire*.

You will find similar people who will keep moving from one social media platform to another in search of the best platform. Just as I recommend finding the right direct selling company, you should also look for the right social media platform and once you have found the right fit, you must use all your focus and commitment to build your brand on that platform.

My goal for you in this chapter is to help you master the fundamental concepts that you can use to analyze the suitability of any social media platform for you. Once you understand how to apply the psychology behind the process of brand building and selling, you can do it on any platform, today or in the future. Whatever you do, never forget your purpose – making genuine connections with people, irrespective of the platform. At the same time, you need to understand how different platforms operate, what works best on each of the platforms, the different kinds of content needed for different platforms and who goes to which platform and for what. This fundamental clarity will take you ahead and keep you ahead.

> *"The size of your audience doesn't matter. What's important is that your audience is listening."*
> — RANDY PAUSCH

Let's quickly discuss the key features of some of the most popular platforms. We have chosen platforms that are popular right now and this list may change in the future. Please understand that I don't just want your knowledge to be limited to a few trending platforms; I want to empower you with the science behind operating any social media platform so that you can work confidently on any other platform in the future. The concepts that we are learning in this chapter today are universal in nature and you can apply the same to analyze any social media platform.

#Facebook

It's the number one social media platform with 279 crore active users across the globe, which translates to almost one-third of the world population. With 31 crore active users, India is the #1 country for Facebook in terms of number of active users.* People in all age groups use Facebook. Content is generally in the form of images and videos. Posting is easy and fast. People come to Facebook looking for people because it is very easy to search for people here.

It has several options to engage and stay connected with followers like easy commenting, livestreaming and stories. You can easily move comments and interaction from a public profile to private messaging using Facebook Messenger. Facebook is also one of the most used platforms by advertisers these days. It has a feature wherein you can organize online events with your followers. You can build and nurture your online community with Facebook groups. Many times, people get confused between a Facebook profile, a Facebook page and Facebook groups. Let us understand the basic differences between these three:

Facebook Profile

A profile is a place on Facebook where you can share information about yourself, such as your interests, photos, videos, current city and work. This is how all of us start our Facebook accounts.

---

* https://www.statista.com/statistics/268136/top-15-countries-based-on-number-of-facebook-users/

Facebook Page

A page is a place on Facebook where people, businesses, brands and organizations can connect with their fans or customers. When someone likes or follows a page on Facebook, they can start seeing updates from that page in their News Feed. You must have a profile to create a page. When your profile crosses 5,000 friends, it has to be converted to a page, but there is no limit for the number of followers of a page. A lot of analytics and insights are also available on your Facebook page that are not available on your profile. You can easily convert your profile to a page at any time to get those insights and analytics even if the number of friends on your page is less than 5,000.

Facebook Group

A Facebook group is a place to communicate about shared interests with specific people. You can create a group for anything – your family reunion, your after-work sports team, your network marketing team, your business team, college alumni, neighbors, work colleagues, book club etc. You can customize the group's privacy settings to decide who you want to be able to join and see the group, who can post, how the comments will be handled etc. It's very easy to add members to or delete members from a group. When anyone joins a group on Facebook, they start seeing content from that group in their News Feed. As you start growing your community and influence on Facebook, you can start creating your own groups. You can create multiple groups, too.

> *"Create something people want to share."*
> — JOHN JANTSCH

#Instagram

With 127 crore-plus active users, Instagram is a popular social media platform, especially for youngsters. As per recent statistics, Instagram is predominantly used by people in the age group of 18-29 and more than 8 crore photos and videos are shared on Instagram every day. Instagram was originally started as a photo sharing app but now you can also share videos in different lengths and formats. Posting is fast and easy. People come to Instagram searching for people. It has several excellent options for engaging with your audience like stories, reels and livestreaming.

There is a unique 'highlights' feature on your Instagram profile that you can use to showcase your achievements, products, lifestyle, connections or anything significant that you want the world to know about. While people can comment publicly on your posts, there is also an amazing private messaging option in the form of DMs (direct messaging). Businesses and brands have also started using Instagram aggressively. Since it's more youth-oriented, you need to have innovation, creativity and authenticity to grab people's attention. Just like with Facebook, you can convert your personal Instagram account to a business account. With a business account, you will be able to access a lot of free built-in insights about your account like post performance, follower activity and many other audience insights.

Since Instagram and Facebook belong to the same parent company, you have got an option where you can choose to show your Instagram posts and stories on Facebook as well, at the click of a button. You can make this as a permanent setting or you can do it post by post. Although both are photo and video-sharing platforms, Facebook offers 3 features which many users find better compared to Instagram:

1. You cannot post more than 10 images on Instagram, but there is no such limit on Facebook.
2. You can add a clickable link in the description below any post or video on Facebook, while you cannot do this on Instagram.
3. You can give your key message or tagline in a cover image on top of your page in Facebook. Instagram doesn't have a cover image option.

#YouTube

Originally started as a video-sharing platform, YouTube has now established itself as the second largest search engine in the world with 300 crore searches every month. As per current statistics, YouTube has 229 crore active users and 100 hours of videos are uploaded on YouTube every minute. People generally don't go to YouTube searching for people; rather, people go to YouTube to search for specific content. How-tos, tutorials, problem solving and educational and subject-specific videos are among the most popular forms of content on YouTube. You can also use the livestreaming feature of YouTube to share your content live with your audience and engage with them in real-time through comments. YouTube has a community section for posting images. You can also post short-duration stories like you post on Facebook or Instagram. They are also testing a short-duration video format called "shorts".

It's a time and resource-intensive platform that is relatively more complicated. It's not just your content but also many other specifics like the caption, thumbnail, tags, description etc. that work to get your content to the top of the search results. In the last few years, it has become one of the favorite digital platforms for advertisers as well. The results that you get for your search on YouTube may sometimes be driven by paid advertisements, and the video you see at the top of the search results may be made not by the best person on that subject, but rather by the best marketer. All the videos on your channel can be seen at any point of time and any video can appear on the top of the search results as per the changing algorithms. As people can watch any video at any time based on the topic they are looking for, it's really tough to track comments.

Engagement is limited with the audience as it is generally a one-sided sharing of content. It has become too cluttered and competitive these days.

#LinkedIn

LinkedIn is a professional network for career-oriented people and is used predominantly by people in the age group of 30-54 years. You will generally find serious content related to career growth, jobs, skill development, training and entrepreneurship here. Most of the content is professional in nature and people generally don't share entertainment, travel or personal life photos on LinkedIn. Connection with others is possible but there is limited interaction and a lower number of active users. You can post articles, infographics and videos related to your career and professional life. LinkedIn is also used by corporates for hiring and by professionals for networking. You can get good-quality prospects for direct selling on LinkedIn.

#Twitter

Twitter is more like a message broadcasting platform generally used by people in the age group of 24-40 years. The majority of content is text, how-to articles or listicles. Twitter is best for sharing news, PR items and current matters. Different experts have different recommendations in terms of how many tweets should be made every day, but you can decide your own number of daily tweets based on the time available and how often you can produce good-quality tweets in a day. Each tweet has a limit on the number of characters. You can also send DMs on Twitter and you can add not just text but also images, videos or gifs.

#Pinterest

Pinterest is an image sharing platform and posts are called pins here. The majority age group is 30-49 years and almost 80% of Pinterest's users are female. Most of the content is graphic-heavy, high-resolution, high-quality and mostly professionally edited images. Many e-commerce retailers use it for driving traffic and leads. The recommended posting frequency is 30 pins per day.

#Snapchat

Snapchat is primarily a photo-sharing platform but you can upload 10-second videos and business promotion material as well. A unique feature of Snapchat is their ever-growing set of best-in-the-industry filters that allow the users to let their imaginations run wild while editing photos. New, crazy filters are added regularly but the photos you post are auto-deleted within 24 hours. You have no record of what you have shared and you don't even know if the target audience has watched your photos or videos. You also have the direct messaging option to connect with people.

> *"Starting and being consistent and not giving up is more important than being brilliant."*
> — MARK SCHAEFER

As we wrap up this chapter, I would like to remind you that being a direct seller, your primary goal for building your social media brand is to speed up the accomplishment of your business goals. So whichever social media platform you choose must have these three features:

1. Simple and duplicable

In the direct selling business, we don't do great things; we do things that are duplicable. So choose a platform where your teammates can also easily open accounts and interact with each other.

2. KLT rule

Your social media platform should make it easier and faster for people to Like you, Know you and Trust you.

3. Ease of conversation

The results you get from a social media platform depend on conversations and not on the number of followers. So choose a platform that offers ease of conversation.

During my social media journey I have fallen in love with one word that has been my best ally. That word is 'experiment'. When in doubt, experiment and the results will guide you towards the right way. If you are confused between two platforms or any two or three different activities, just experiment and your followers will guide you to the right solution.

During this social media journey, use happiness as your compass. Fall in love with the process. If you are just chasing business goals, you will miss out on all the fun you can have while building your social media brand and the huge impact that you can have on a countless number of people. Happy socializing.

> *"I alone cannot change the world, but I can cast a stone across the waters to create many ripples."*
> — MOTHER TERESA

REMEMBER AND SHARE

- No social media platform is good or bad; you need to identify which platform will give you the best results.
- While you can build your brand on multiple platforms, spend the most time on the platform that has the type of people you are most trying to attract and where you are getting the best results.
- Nothing is permanent on social media. Keep moving as per the trends and audience.
- Choose a platform where it is easy to build connections, have conversations and engage with your audience.
- Choose a social media platform that is simple and duplicable.

KEY ACTIONS TO TAKE

- If you have not yet decided your top 2 social media platforms that you want to seriously build on, decide right now and start working on building your brand there.

All the data given in this chapter has been taken from statista.com. Other sources used:

- https://www.statista.com/statistics/471370/us-adults-who-use-social-networks-age/
- https://aofund.org/resource/choosing-right-social-media-platform-your-business/

CHAPTER 10

11 Strategies for Creating Engaging and Eye-Catching Posts

"All one needs is a computer, a network connection, and a bright spark of initiative and creativity to join the economy."
— Don Tapscott

POSTS ARE THE QUICKEST way to connect with your audience. They are fast to create and quicker to post. Your audience can instantly get your message in one single glance. But creating engaging posts is an art as well as a science. I call it an art because you can use all your creativity and ideas to design your posts in your own style. You are the owner of your account and you have the flexibility to design your posts the way you like. Designing posts is also a science, because there are certain principles that must be followed while designing one. I leave the creativity and innovation part to you but will share with you 11 key principles for making engaging and eye-catching posts. Master these principles and apply them with your own unique style to build your community on social media.

#1. Never break the KISS principle

KISS is one of the classic communication principles that I have been teaching in my workshops for more than a decade. You can use it in all areas of your life and if you can adopt this as a guiding principle while designing your posts, you will never go wrong with your posts. KISS is easy to remember – Keep It Short and Simple.

It has been said that one picture is worth a thousand words. Good posts are all about a visual and one key message. Never write too many messages. One heading with one sub-heading is enough. The text should not take more than one-third of the space on your post. A simple rule of thumb is that a post should be self-explanatory – you shouldn't need to give any explanation to convey your message. The best posts are the kind where your audience gets what you want to say just by giving them one glance. Avoid jargon and complicated words. Use language that your audience can easily understand.

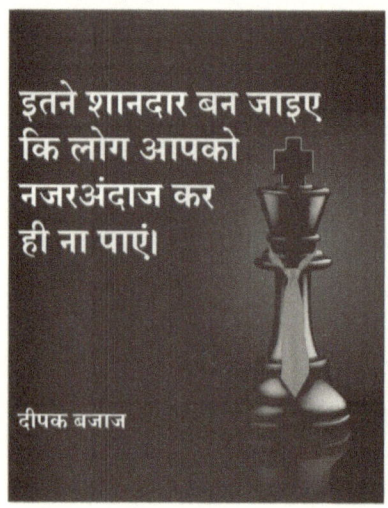

#2. Use the R³MAT Test

R³MAT is the underlying goal of all advertising and marketing campaigns. If most of your posts pass the R³MAT test, you will get massive results from all your social media efforts.

R³MAT = Giving the Right Message to the Right Audience at the Right Time

That is actually the real objective of every post – to deliver the right message to your audience. So quickly check with R³MAT before posting any content.

> *"I use social media as an idea generator, trend mapper and strategic compass for all of our online business ventures."*
> — PAUL BARRON

#3. Use easily readable fonts

However tempted you may feel to use stylish and fancy fonts, please remember that simple and easily readable fonts have the maximum impact. Most of the people access social media on their mobile phones where images look very small and when these posts are viewed in a grid, they look even smaller. So while choosing fonts for your posts, avoid fancy fonts that are stylish but tough to read. Use fonts that can be read from a distance. In fact, you can experiment with different fonts and finalize a few fonts that give you the best effect. Use these fonts to create a favorite collection of fonts that you can repeatedly use in your posts so that any time you create a post, you don't need to do a fresh search for fonts. Just go to your collection and pick up the best one.

The background of the post also affects the readability of the text. Use simple backgrounds that highlight the text.

#4. Don't use more than 3 colors in one post

As a general rule, don't use more than 3 colors in one post. It becomes confusing. The choice of colors depends on the kind of brand image you want to portray. When you continue to use a certain fixed set of colors for your posts over a period of time, they become a part of your brand identity as well. After some time, people will recognize your posts just by looking at that color combination. Continue experimenting with different patterns and styles to give variety and add a greater impact to your message.

#5. Use photo editing and poster making apps

You can add a spark to your posts with some photo editing apps and make them appear professional. There are so many apps that are easy to use and have preset templates that you can use to design excellent-quality posts really fast. Some of the apps that I have used and found good are as follows:

- InShot – Perfect for new users. Super easy to use and gives you a lot of flexibility and styling options.
- Canva – It has preset templates for poster designing, Instagram stories, YouTube stories and Instagram and YouTube community posts.
- Adobe Lightroom
- Snapseed

The list is endless. There are countless apps available and many more are launched every day. Keep trying new ones.

Install new ones, keep them if you love them and uninstall them immediately if you don't like the features and designs they offer. Each app has certain unique features. Keep a set of the most suitable apps on your phone. Use styles and features from different ones to have a variety of design options.

#6. Choose filters carefully

Every time you update your social media apps, one thing you are sure to find is some new filters. Both the social media platforms and designing apps offer you a wide range of filters. Filters are a quick and amazing way to add style and variety to your photos. Instagram and Snapchat offer some of the best in-built filters. But filters will work for you only if your selection of them is good. Just like all those designer clothes that look great on a dummy in a showroom window but may not actually look good on you when you wear them at home, there are many fancy filters that look great when you see them but may not work for your brand. Use filters that go with your style and also enhance the beauty of your posts.

> *"Design is not just what it looks like and feels like. Design is how it works."*
>
> — STEVE JOBS

#7. Make posts that appeal to your audience

One of the biggest disadvantages of the internet is that it is full of free advice and most of it has been written by people who don't have any real experience of doing the activity or don't have good accounts themselves. Every other minute you will find a new blog, YouTube video, podcast or ebook teaching you how to make viral posts. Be really careful, as many of these articles are written by people who are struggling to get even 50 views on their articles or videos.

Anyway, let others do whatever they are doing; just don't be tempted to try every new idea you read about. You have your own audience and you know what works for them. Experimenting once in a while is amazing but experimenting with every alternate post will confuse your audience and they will leave you out of frustration and disappointment. Be clear about who your audience is and make posts that appeal to them.

Scroll through your social media insights or converse with your audience through comments or stories to find out and to validate what interests them the most. Then create content based on their needs that they can relate to.

#8. Make your page real and personal

Sometimes we get so engrossed with systems and patterns that we forget that what is special about your page is you. Although we are interacting with each other through devices, ultimately it's one human connecting with another. So give a personal touch to your page. Add your energy and presence to your page. Use as many photos of yours as you can – photos always connect more than infographics. You can see the effect of your personal photos immediately through the number of likes and comments. Other than your photos, you can share photos of interesting things like a book, an article, a particular image or paragraph from a book, a poster, an event photo etc. You can share BTS (behind the scenes) photos too. They give a personal touch to your profile and add life to it.

#9. Look for inspiration

Look for trends and ideas from thought leaders, industry icons and your favorite influencers. You don't need to create trends but if you can just keep your eyes and ears open, you will spot new trends. Try to adopt new trends or styles in your posts as that will keep your posts fresh and dynamic. If you use a new feature in your posts that any social media platform is promoting, you will get massive organic reach without spending any money.

#10. Multiple posts in one single post

Sometimes, when you want to share multiple points related to one single topic or theme, you can create multiple posts with a similar design and share them together as one post. You can include images as well as videos in these posts and such posts are specifically called carousel posts on Instagram, Twitter and LinkedIn. While the user will see only one image at a time, he or she can swipe to see the other related images in the post. On a Facebook feed, the users will see 3-4 photos in a grid and once they click on it, they can see all the photos or videos one by one. Principally, all the posts are created with similar designs, patterns or color schemes.

Carousel posts add an element of surprise and convey longer messages or a set of points in the best way. Content like 3 ways to X, 5 solutions to X, 6 quick hacks for X, 8 ideas to X and so on are best represented through carousel posts.

#11. Give people what they need

Use Google Trends to find out the most searched terms related to the topic you want to create your content on. Apply filters like region, days etc. and experiment with sub-topics to make your searches better. Use this data to create content that covers the rising or top trends in your industry. You can also relate your content to daily Twitter trends to make it more relevant and engaging.

Following these eleven principles may not guarantee that your posts will be viral but I am sure you will not go wrong if you work with these principles.

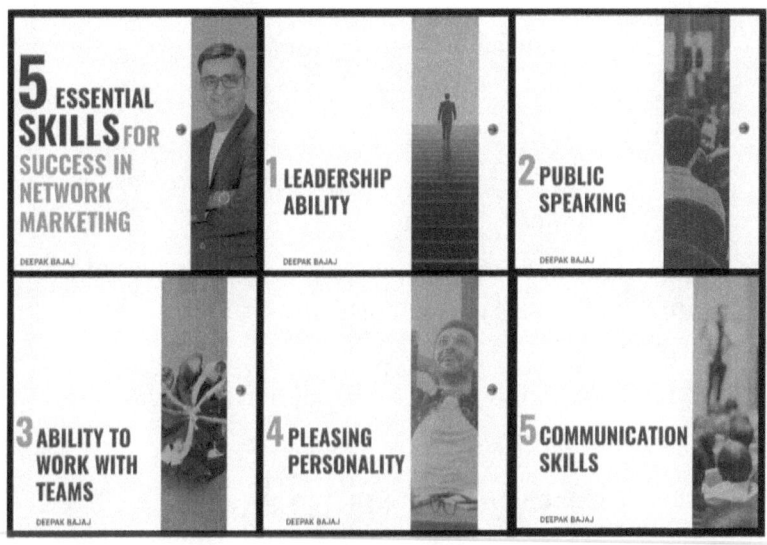

"Here's everything you need to know about creating killer content in 3 simple words: clear, concise and compelling."
— DEMIAN FARNWORTH

REMEMBER AND SHARE

- Posts are the quickest way to convey your message to the audience.
- Posts are different from advertisements. Keep them short and simple.
- A post should be self-explanatory on the first glance.
- Be very clear about your audience and your purpose for creating a post.
- Easy readability is key. Choose fonts, colors and backgrounds accordingly.
- Your regular and BTS photos bring life and emotion to your social media posts and profile. Use them often.
- Be creative. Give your audience variety and surprise them periodically.

KEY ACTIONS TO TAKE

- Analyze the posts you have shared in the last few weeks and identify a few mistakes that you have been making.
- Based on today's lesson, what are the top 5 changes you will implement in your posts from today?
- Make a post on your learnings from this chapter and share it with your friends and community.

CHAPTER 11

14 Expert Secrets for Making Impactful Videos on a Low Budget

"Authenticity, honesty and personal voice underlie much of what's successful on the web."

— RICK LEVINE

AMONG ALL THE CONTENT that you can create, videos are by far the best way to present your content and connect with the audience. Videos have more life and energy that help your audience connect better with your message. They have more emotions than any image, post or written content and people are comparatively more focused while watching videos. Videos work the best accordingly to the KLT rule too. When people hear you and see you, they are more likely to feel that they Know you, Like you and Trust you. In recent years, I have repeatedly observed that videos are generally found to score more in terms of all key numbers – likes, comments and shares. All these factors have made videos the most preferred form of content these days and video making has become an absolutely essential skill to master.

I don't know how good you are at making videos today. Are you comfortable in front of a camera or not? You may be scared and may have a lot of doubts, like, "I don't know how to do it", "I don't look good on camera", "I don't have a good setup", "I don't have anything great to share", "My language is not perfect", "People may not like my videos" etc. Before we get into the technicalities of video making, I want you to understand and remember these two things that have been my guiding principles for life that I have applied in every area of my life:

Guiding Principle #1 –
Feel the fear and do it anyway

Fear is natural and everyone feels it. Many times, fear is a message from your subconscious to prepare more. Accept the fear and feel the fear but still go ahead and do whatever you need to do. This has been my mantra since my school days. Every time I got a chance to do something I had never done before, I raised my hand and said "yes". Did I feel fear? Yes. All the time. But I never allowed fear to stop me from doing what I always wanted to do in my life.

I was in Macau, China a few years ago to do the world's highest bungee jump. You have to buy tickets for the bungee jump on the ground floor and afterwards you take the elevator to the top of the Macau Tower for the jump. It's 764 feet above the ground. There is a cord or rope attached to your feet and you just jump from the designated place. Walking towards the jumping platform, standing on its edge for a few minutes and watching the depth below was very scary in itself. And for the next few seconds I was in the air, falling like a stone towards the ground. Was it scary? Don't even ask that question. I was scared as hell. I smiled for the photos, but if you see the video of that jump you can easily make out my fear beneath that fake smile. My instructor told me to jump and it took me a few more seconds to gather all my courage and jump.

Guess what happened after I completed the jump and landed safely on the ground? My head was still spinning and it took me more than 20 minutes to feel normal. But one more thing happened. I got my certificate for completing the

Guinness Book of World Records-certified highest bungee jump. That certificate had my name printed on it and my photos of the jump. I felt proud of myself for beating my fear. I took a photo of the certificate and emailed it to my children. I was a winner. I felt like the unstoppable Deepak Bajaj.

What did I do next? I went to Dubai and booked a skydive, and this time the jumping height was not 764 feet but 13,000 feet. You board an aircraft and when you are in the sky at 13,000 feet above the ground, they open the doors of the aircraft and you jump out. Buildings look like matchboxes. Cars and buses look like ants. Was jumping out of that airplane scary? Yes, it was. What else would you feel if you were holding the door handle of an open door of an aircraft at 13,000 feet? I was scared as hell. I was literally frozen with fear. Trust me, I was not laughing when I jumped. But I still jumped. It felt like the end of the world for the first 2-3 seconds. We were falling down like a rock at an unimaginable speed. You have to experience it to really understand what 'freefall' means.

But after a few seconds the parachute opened, a cool breeze was kissing my face and I was flying like a bird. It was an out-of-this-world feeling. So serene and surreal. I didn't feel like coming down to the ground. I wanted this experience to continue forever. Now make a guess. What did I achieve after this jump? I had overcome my fear again. I had won over my fear again. My self-belief and confidence shot up like crazy and I had etched in my heart once again that I was unstoppable and I could do anything.

I didn't stop there. I travelled to Bali, Indonesia to go scuba diving. I was in the middle of the sea and my instructor told me to jump into the sea. Trust me, jumping into the sea is a totally different experience than jumping into a swimming pool. I was frozen and could not move. After I had mustered the courage to jump, as soon as I went under the water, I felt that I would choke to death and my instructors pulled me out of the water. This happened 3 times. From my fourth dive onwards, I gradually started settling down and it took me half a day to be comfortable underwater. But I was determined to win over that fear so I continued to dive until I knew I was not fearful of it any more. Guess what this did to me again – it upheld my self-belief that I am bigger than any of my fears. It reconfirmed that I could do anything if I set my eyes on it.

I felt fear not just with adventure sports but also every time I started something new in my life. Going from my town to South India for studies, starting a network marketing business, resigning my job to pursue my business, changing cities, starting my YouTube channel, writing my first book, sharing my first post on Instagram, launching my online program, starting my training and consulting company, going for training events costing me lakhs of rupees – all of these felt scary at first. I had my share of doubts and insecurities but what changed my life was taking action in spite of feeling the fear.

Please understand that the only way to eliminate fear is to do what you are scared of. Do it so many times that your conscious and subconscious mind both forget that you were full of fear someday. My coach Tony Robbins always says this: "Massive action in the face of fear is the only way to success." So feel the fear and do it anyway. Every time you do it, you make your faith stronger than your fear. Keep making your faith stronger and stay unstoppable.

Guiding Principle #2 –
Preparation is the best solution for any problem

Let me repeat again that often, fear is a message from the subconscious that you need to prepare more.

One of my favorite football coaches of all time, the legendary Vince Lombardi, once said, *"The will to win is not nearly as important as the will to prepare to win. Most people have the will to win. Everyone enjoys winning and everything that comes with it. The people who are willing to put in the hard work required to prepare for a long period of time are more rare. Great performers have that rare will to prepare."*

If you feel you could not make good videos so far, it was probably because you never invested your time into learning how to. If you make it a priority now to learn video making, I am sure you could change your game really fast. So commit to it now.

Let us establish one fact: video making is not an option; it is mandatory if you want to establish your brand on social media. If you want more and more people to connect with you, see your message and spread your message, then videos are the most effective way to do so.

The good news is that video making is totally a learnable skill and it is as intuitive and easy as walking. Have you seen teenagers and youngsters making such creative videos from their phones and editing them within minutes? A whole technological ecosystem is supporting you to do this. You just need to learn the way of making effective and impactful videos on a low budget and in less time. That's exactly what you will learn in this chapter today.

Principally, there are 6 components of great video making as shown in Illustration 6. If you can take care of these 6 components while making your videos, you will never go wrong. Explaining all these 6 components in detail would fill a book in itself, so I am sharing 14 of the most important insights and techniques below for making effective and impactful videos on a low budget in little time.

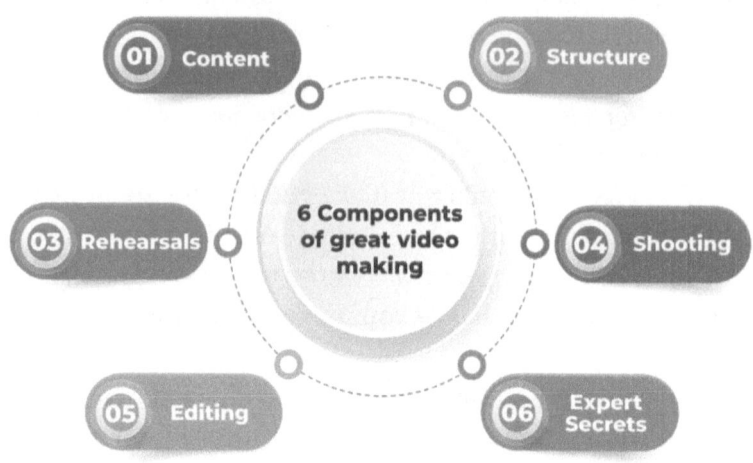

Illustration 6

Source – *Social Media and Online Business Mastery*, an online training course by Deepak Bajaj.

#1. Rule of three

While you can cover any number of learnings or key points in a video, my training and coaching experience with 10 lakh-plus participants has repeatedly proved that one should not include more than 3 key learnings or takeaways in one single video. So decide on your 3 key deliverables for any video and prepare your content, examples, studies, statistics, stories and all the other data to validate and strengthen those 3 points. If your audience can remember those 3 points after the video, you have done an excellent job.

#2. Start with short videos

Long is not always good. People's attention spans have been decreasing rapidly and it is becoming tougher by the day to grab and hold people's attention on social media. Hence it is advisable to make short videos, especially when you are starting out. Make your videos so compelling that people continue watching them with full attention.

> *"Your videos should not be long but your message and impact should not be long forgotten."*
> — Deepak Bajaj

Longer videos will need more time and effort for conceptualizing, content writing and editing. So if you are a beginner, instead of working on 10 tips or 7 ideas, stick to 2-3 key points and give your audience good value for the time that they invest into your videos.

#3. Never underestimate the value of good-quality content

I have already mentioned in a previous chapter that content really matters a lot. Good thumbnails and captions can get people to your video, but people will be glued to your video solely on the merit of your content. Work hard to make good content. I am fascinated with the power of content; that's why I have included an exclusive chapter in this book focusing on it. Any content can be considered good only when it serves its audience. It should give provide excellent value and give solutions to the audience.

> *"Content is fire. Social media is gasoline."*
> — Jay Baer

#4. Never work for a viral video

This is a big mental block that sometimes comes in the way of creating good-quality content. The biggest mistake any content creator can make, in my opinion, is to shift their focus from trying to make value-adding content to making viral content. Life is all about focus and intention. This shift in focus looks small and insignificant but its impact is huge and felt by everyone. When your focus is to create viral content, you will start looking around for what sells, what gets more likes or more views, what is latest and trending etc. Your desperation to find this would take you from one article to another and one social media account to another, in the end leaving you so confused and frustrated that you would either close your account or produce content so bad that nobody would watch it.

Every social media creator has a unique audience and brand image. Everyone is working in their niche and they are making content for that particular niche. When you start copying them without actually knowing the whole picture, you end up nowhere.

As a matter of fact, no one knows at the time of making a video whether it will go viral or not. I have already shared the example of my own YouTube channel. There are videos with 10 lakh views and there are videos with similar topics that struggle to reach even 50,000 views. Your key task is to produce excellent content that adds value. How far this video will reach will be decided by many factors beyond your control. Stay focused on serving your audience and not doing what looks popular or seems like a shortcut to fame.

#5. Follow the right structure for maximum impact

However good your content is, you still need to present it in the right structure and sequence for maximum impact. Haphazard presentation will confuse your audience and will not get you the desired results. After researching some of the best videos and experimenting with different structures, I have found a structure that has served me well for so many years. Thousands of my online course participants have also got excellent results with the same. So here is my recommended sequence for presenting your ideas in a video:

a. A quick introduction

Just say your name and a greeting. Do this even if it is your 100th video.

b. Powerful opening

Give people a compelling reason as to why should they watch your video. Tell them right in the beginning what benefit you are going to deliver or what problem you are going to solve through the video.

c. Main content

Prepare your core content as per the guidelines you have got from the chapter on content creation.

d. Call to action

What do you want them to do after watching the video?

> *"Ordinary people with commitment can make an extraordinary impact on the world."*
> — JOHN C. MAXWELL

#6. Rehearsals

Rehearsals are absolutely important before shooting any video. Even if you think you are the biggest expert in the field, I highly recommend a rehearsal before you shoot the video. Make a quick demo video on your mobile phone and check a few basic things like choice of words, voice tonality and, most importantly, timing. Most of the time, you will realize that you are either finishing too soon or talking way longer than you originally planned. I have experienced this so many times with my live events' participants – just 10 minutes of rehearsal can improve the quality of your video by 3-5 times.

#7. Lighting

Lighting is the most important but most taken-for-granted element while shooting a video. You need to add a good amount of lighting while going live or while shooting any video. Good lighting makes a video look professional and, more importantly, people will feel like watching it. Ask yourself – would you watch a video for more than a few seconds if you struggled to see the speaker? No, you wouldn't. Then how do you expect your audience to watch your video with bad-quality lighting?

Even the best of cameras will not give excellent results without adequate lighting. Professionals add extra lights even during daylight shoots. Principally, the better the lighting, the better the video quality is. Remember this rule of thumb – whenever you are in doubt, add some more lights. I am not expecting you to go for expensive studio lights but a good-quality ring light, T-light or a few LED bulbs are enough to give you a good-quality video.

I recommend you set up one or two fixed places for shooting videos so that any time you need to shoot a video, you can just go there and shoot it. Experiment with different lighting and backgrounds and make a fixed setup so that it saves you from having to recreate the setup every time. You can keep one or two fixed lights and keep another one or two as portable lights that you can add whenever you need.

#8. Good microphone

Even if people love you and your content is awesome, if people are struggling to hear what you are saying or the voice volume is low or not clear, they will immediately move to some other video. Good sound is absolutely essential for a good video. Don't rely on the in-built mic of your phone; always use a good-quality external mic. A good mic for beginners does not cost more than 1,000 rupees. For many years, I have used a basic Boya mic (model BYM1 Omnidirectional Lavalier Condenser Microphone) that cost me just 600 rupees and provided amazing quality for hundreds of videos. Keep an extra mic and batteries as a backup if you are creating content regularly.

#9. Background

Your background also makes a big difference to the quality of your video. Generally speaking, a clean wall in light colors or plain curtains works the best. If you are shooting at home, make sure to clean up the area that will appear in the background of the video. You can keep 2-3 sets of curtains in different colors to add variety to the videos. If you want to experiment with different video backgrounds, you can use a bright green colored screen in the backdrop to utilize a popular technique called chroma keying. When you shoot a video with a green screen, you can easily use the chroma keying feature present in most editing software to change the background to anything you like.

#10. Shoot long videos in short clips

I have seen some people struggling to shoot the entire video, and that too without any errors, in one single take. It's lovely if you can do that, but don't make it a self-imposed punishment. It's not necessary to shoot the entire video in one go. Constantly speaking in front of the camera may be tiring for your body and voice. Take breaks, drink some water and review your script. Shoot short clips and merge them later while editing. You can keep the key points in front of you too if you need to. I can give you a quick hack if you want to take breaks while shooting. Let's say you are covering three points in one video – complete one point and take a break. This will also make editing easier and faster.

#11. Shoot in the right aspect ratio

The aspect ratio of an image or video is the ratio of its width to its height. It is commonly expressed as two numbers separated by a colon, as in 16:9. Every social media platform has a preferred aspect ratio for its content. For getting the best response, it is highly recommended that you post the content in the aspect ratio that is most appropriate for that particular social media platform. A quick look at Illustration 7 will clarify the concept of different aspect ratios.

Of course, you can adjust the aspect ratio while editing the video, but smart video makers decide on the aspect ratio before shooting the video. You already know where you are going to post that particular video, so why not shoot it in accordance with the platform you'll be posting it on? This also makes the editing work a lot easier. Why shoot a portrait video for YouTube when you know that landscape videos

Illustration 7

will look the best on that platform? Here are the current aspect ratios for some of the most popular platforms as of today. You can verify it periodically, as things keep changing fast on social media.

- YouTube videos – 16:9
- Regular Instagram videos – 4:5 or 1:1
- IGTV videos and Instagram reels – 9:16
- Facebook – 16:9 or 9:16

#12. Video editing

Good editing enhances the quality and visual appeal of your videos. Editing does the same for your video that gift-wrapping does for a good gift. While you can post videos without any editing, I recommend you edit every video because it enhances the user experience. Many people are scared of editing because they believe it is a highly technical skill. First of all, get out of this mental block that editing is a tough job and that you need to be a certified video editor to create good-quality video. Unless you are a big corporate brand or a big social media influencer, you actually don't need any fancy editing. I even know some big social media influencers who do basic editing on their videos, and their videos reach out to millions. There are so many mobile apps and software packages that are really easy to use and have been designed for people who are amateurs at editing.

If you shoot the video with the right lighting, right placement of the camera, good mic and the right backdrop, you will only need minimum editing. Most of the time, you will either need to cut some portions or merge some short clips together. You can use ready-made templates to add text in videos. Royalty-free images and video footage are also available in abundance all over the internet.

Thousands of mobile apps are available with amazing features that anyone can use without any prior experience. I know that newer and better apps are being launched every day and you must keep trying different ones. Some of the free apps that I have been using for quite a long time for video editing are InShot, KineMaster and FilmoraGo.

#13. Maintain ESPN in your videos

This is one of the favorite formulas among participants from my *Social Media and Online Business Mastery* course. I have summarized four key things that you must add to your video in the word ESPN. ESPN stands for Energy, Spark, Passion and your Natural Style. Irrespective of the social media platform and type of content you are shooting, you must deliver the video with these four key components. They give life and energy to your video.

> *"Value-adding content delivered with energy and passion can fuel a revolution."*
> — DEEPAK BAJAJ

#14. Never compare your work with anyone else's

This is last but not least. I have chosen to include this in the list of 14 insights and expert secrets that I have shared with you in this chapter because many people who can do amazing work on social media and who can be a great inspiration for so many people just get frustrated by comparing their work with some other big leader or veteran social media influencer. Many times, these really good people quit because they feel their work is smaller or inferior compared to that of others. Trust me, no work is small if it is done with the right intention to help others.

Don't get intimidated by big YouTubers or industry leaders and never try to imitate their content and style.

You don't know when they started or how their audience and channel evolved. Many big YouTubers got popular not just because of their content but also because of being the early starters. There are many others who are professional YouTubers or social media influencers and they have been building their accounts 24/7 with a full-fledged professional team. You don't know their objectives or strategy.

You have specific results to be achieved from social media. You have your own unique message and unique audience to serve. Stay focused on the same. Anyway, you cannot compare your first-grade performance with somebody's eighth-grade or tenth-grade performance. Everyone has his or her own race. Start off right now and give it your best efforts. Tomorrow, you and your social media page could be a big source of hope, insight and inspiration for many others.

Although I have shared in this book all the key concepts that are absolutely essential to begin your social media transformation journey, I still think the best way to learn video making is actually through a video. If you have the passion and commitment to explore these concepts in deeper details, I invite you to explore my *Social Media and Online Business Mastery* program which is a one-of-a-kind, complete, result-oriented and very affordable course which has helped direct sellers across the world build big businesses online.

In the end, I would like to remind you that video making is purely a learnable skill and you will master it as you make more and more videos. Now you know all the key concepts and I am sure you will get amazing results once you start applying them to your videos. Make some awesome videos and share them with me and our community too. I am super excited to see you as a video superstar.

"Genius is in the idea. Impact, however, comes from action."
— Simon Sinek

REMEMBER AND SHARE

- Never forget the rule of 3 – don't include more than 3 key takeaways or learnings in one single video.
- The best of content will not deliver great results if you don't present it in the right sequence.
- A good opening and an effective CTA (call to action) multiplies the impact and results from a video.
- 10 minutes of rehearsal can improve the quality of your video by 3-5 times.
- Ensure there is adequate lighting, a good mic, the right backdrop and proper height and placement before the video shoot.
- Maintain ESPN in your videos – Energy, Spark, Passion and Natural Style.
- Never compare yourself with any other YouTuber, big leader or big social media account.

KEY ACTIONS TO TAKE

- Watch the last 10 videos that you posted on social media and identify what could you have done better.
- Make your own video making strategy based on today's lesson.
- Make a video today on the top 3 best learnings from today's chapter and share the same with your friends and community.

CHAPTER 12

Secret Formulas of the World's Best Social Media Influencers

"If you want to be the best, you have to do things that other people aren't willing to do."

— Michael Phelps

I TRUST YOU 100%. I believe you have the seeds of greatness inside you. You are a powerhouse of talent, potential, energy and commitment. You can achieve anything you set your eyes on. This chapter in this book is a proof of my trust in you. In this book, I have already covered everything you need to make it big with social media and I was wondering whether I should cover this topic on the secrets of top 1% of leaders or not. But I have done it because I truly believe greatness is everybody's birthright. Every legend started from zero one day. Today is the first day of the rest of your life. Be absolutely committed to do everything it takes to achieve everything you dreamt of. I have taken this chapter from my most popular global online program, *Social Media and Online Business Mastery*. It's a 3-week program for total social media and online business-building mastery and this chapter is one part of what I cover in day 13 of that course.

Please remember that the top 1% of people in every industry were also a part of the remaining 99% at some point of time. They just worked on developing the mindset, skillset and toolset required for massive success and that brought them to the top 1%. So wherever you are today, if you are committed to learn and grow, you will always stay unstoppable.

Once you profile is set and you've started creating and posting useful content consistently, the next goal should be to multiply the effectiveness and results of your social media efforts. This chapter is dedicated to taking you to the top of your game by giving you insights on what the top 1% of people do differently from others. For your understanding, I have given it the acronym CARE – Conversations, Analytics, Relationships and End Result. So top leaders CARE more than others. Let's understand these 4 elements of CARE.

How the world's best social media influencers CARE for their followers

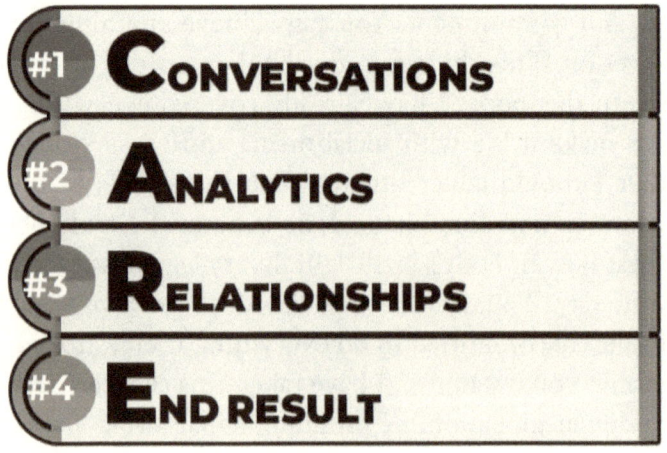

Illustration 8

"Care about your customers more than about yourself, and you'll do well."
— Derek Sivers

#1. Conversations

Conversation is the heart of leadership. This is the key requirement for success on social media and is especially important if you want to recruit and manage a big team online. The top 1% of leaders are masters of conversation and communication. They have understood the formula for massive results from social media:

Posting + Conversation = Massive Results

So remember that posting alone is not enough. Even robots can do the posting using the best strategies and algorithms. Sharing a nice picture, writing a few nice words and using some relevant hashtags are all important, but they will never lead to any results if you don't do the critical part of conversations. The results lie in conversation.

If you agree that conversations are important, please understand the other thing about conversations. There are two types of conversations on social media:

1. Reactive conversation

Replying to comments and incoming mentions or answering DMs are a reactive form of conversation. Someone else started a conversation or asked a question and you answered. This is absolutely important and considered good social media etiquette.

2. Proactive conversation

This is your winning edge and this is where you will get your next set of leaders. You don't wait for people to comment or send you a private message. You start new conversations with your followers and with strangers. You can either start a conversation with people who like your posts or tap into relevant conversations. You can spark a new conversation with people who may be talking about you or your brand or something about the industry you are in. If someone comments on an industry leader's post, you could start off a conversation there too.

Don't consider conversation as a punishment. Take out the time and talk to people joyfully. Remember, gold lies in conversations and engagement.

Engagement

When you interact one-on-one with your audience, it is generally called conversation, but when you interact with several people with a single post or video, it is called engagement in social media parlance. All the likes, shares, comments and saves on your posts are cumulatively called engagement. Engagement is one of the key measures of how much your audience loves you and how effective your content is. Hence increasing engagement should be one of your key goals on social media.

The top 1% of leaders continuously do activities that multiply engagement on their page. Your value-adding content is your best bet to make your followers engage with your page but along with that, you can also consider doing some of these activities to increase engagement on your page:

- Ask questions from your audience and make them participate. There is a special tool available on Instagram stories for asking questions.
- Encourage your followers to create some content related to your work and you could highlight some of their best work on your page.
- Hold some giveaways.
- Go live once in a while with one or two of your followers.

- Encourage and share UGC (user-generated content).
- Keep posting stories on Facebook and Instagram. Every time you post a new story, your profile picture appears on the top panel of the home screen of the app for your followers. Stories help you establish your brand presence too.

#2. Analytics

Consistent monitoring and evaluation of your posts and social media page is absolutely essential for the growth of your account. You must have heard me say this before – whatever gets monitored gets improved. So don't just post; check how your posts are doing too. This simple act of checking how your posts are doing is called analytics. If you have a business account, you can go to the analytics section of your profile and you will get a lot of information about who is watching your content and when, whether people are taking actions on your posts etc. Even if you don't look at the deeper analytics, you must keep track of the parameters below to know the pulse of your social media account:

- Likes
- Comments
- Shares
- Reposts
- Link clicks
- Views
- New followers
- Saves
- Mentions

Broadly speaking, your social media strategy is right if most or all of these parameters are improving on a month-to-month basis for your social media account.

#3. Relationships

Starting and nurturing a relationship with your followers is your primary responsibility. This is one key quality of top leaders and you must learn how to build and nurture relationships on social media. Your relationship with your followers will keep them on your page and will pave the way for you to offer them your business opportunity in future. Here are 5 quick tips for building great relationships:

1. Promptly respond to comments and private messages. Speeding up your response time not only delights your audience but also develops a sense of trust in them towards you. Fix two or three time slots of 10-15 minutes each spread throughout the day to answer comments and private messages.
2. Reward their loyalty with periodic contests and giveaways.
3. Show up and be visible on your page by initiating and contributing to ongoing conversations on your profile to let them know that you are listening and you care.
4. Be open to feedback. Hear out the feedback you receive and make the most of it by acknowledging and adopting some of it into your future work.
5. If you want others to like, share and comment on your content, you need to do the same for them. So be generous with likes and comments.

"If you want to shine like a sun, first burn like a sun."
— A.P.J. Abdul Kalam

#4. End Results

As you get busy creating and posting content, you must never forget the end result that you want to achieve through your social media efforts. When you know your goals, you will continue your efforts. Most people set long-term goals from social media but the top 1% of leaders set not only long-term goals but also daily goals because they understand that daily consistency is the key to success. Progress is perfection.

We want to make social media an extension of you. It should become as easy for you as brushing your teeth or having lunch at your home. I want you to work on social media effortlessly and the best way to achieve this is by starting with some small and easily achievable daily goals. Make it a practice to do something every single day – make some connections or posts, send messages or replies etc.

Reach out to more and more people and then keep reminding them about you and your awesome value-adding content regularly. We want people not to forget you. The more people see and hear from you, the more they realize that you are caring for them and adding value to their life every day with no immediate expectation of a financial future. Once you are able to establish this, it's more likely that they will trust you when you invite them to do business with you. Remember, social media is not about overnight success. It's not a sprint, my friend; it's a marathon.

When you post consistently every day, you also get another advantage that I call the hidden side of success. The more you post, the better you get at posting. With every post, you will get better at delivering value and doing it better, smarter, faster and more efficiently. It improves not only the lives of others but also your ability to help others. Over a period of time, you will be at a place that is beyond the imagination of most people.

What the top 1% of leaders do differently on social media is **CARE – Conversations, Analytics, Relationships and End Results.**

Care for your friends and followers. Never treat them like just a number that adorns your page. They are human beings who also have expectations and aspirations. They are giving you their precious time and attention. Always work with the genuine intention to help them and serve them. You need not explain or write out your intentions; they show in every action of yours. If you care for your audience and give them what they are looking for, you will get back what you are seeking.

Every single tool, insight or technique that I have shared with you in this book is a seed that will one day bloom and make you a great achiever. Every piece of content that I share in my books, videos, online courses or live events, I always create and share with the intention to serve you and empower you to fulfill all your dreams and live a remarkable life. Each word comes from my heart to yours with all my love, blessings and prayers for your massive success. I really wish that you and I together uplift the profession of direct selling and take this industry to altogether new heights.

> *"You can have everything in life you want, if you will just help enough other people get what they want."*
> — Zig Ziglar

REMEMBER AND SHARE

- The top 1% of income earners are ordinary people who have invested time and money into developing their mindset, skillset and toolset.
- Posting + Conversation = Results.
- Don't just post; check how your posts are doing using analytics.
- Show up regularly on your page, take people's feedback and interact with your audience to nurture your relationship.
- Consistency is the key and progress is perfection. Set not only long-term goals for social media but also daily goals.
- With every post, you will get better at delivering value and doing it smarter, faster and more efficiently.

KEY ACTIONS TO TAKE

- Write down 5 key insights or strategies from today's lesson that you want to implement for building your brand on social media.

CHAPTER 13

The Social Media Sales Funnel for Generating Never-Ending Business Online

"Selling to people who actually want to hear from you is more effective than interrupting strangers who don't."

— SETH GODIN

BACK FROM 2013-2016, I was one among those lakhs of direct sellers who kept posting on Facebook in the hopes that I was building my brand and that I would build a big business from social media. I used to count every like and comment on my posts like we count runs during a cricket match. As the number of my followers grew I shifted from a personal profile to a business page. It was such a proud moment announcing to the world that I would now be active on my business page. It felt as if I had won an Olympic gold medal. I was posting consistently, my followers were engaging with my content and I was getting a lot of likes and comments. I was living in a feel-good zone and spending one to two hours every day on social media.

Everything was good, but I didn't get a single sale in many months and that's when I started digging deeper to find out what I was doing wrong. I studied global leaders, interviewed direct sellers who have been successfully using social media for business-building, started taking online courses and read a lot of books, and what I realized was eye-opening – *"If your aim* is to generate business from social media, posting is only 20% of the work. You will never get any results if you don't do the other 80%." I realized that most of my followers on social media were my existing teammates and getting some 10,000 followers from lakhs of my teammates was not a big achievement anyway.

Just think for a minute about the long sales process we follow for converting strangers to teammates. We make lists, go prospecting, approach prospects, share the opportunity or products with them, follow through and close the sales to get people into our team.

Many of these people are ones we already know and most of this work is face-to-face. Building credibility face-to-face is a little easier than doing it online on social media. But what I was expecting from social media was that total strangers would come into my team just by seeing my posts. I don't know about you, but I have seen lakhs of people who feel the same way and keep posting on social media for years in the hopes of finding their diamond one day.

The rule is simple, my friend – if you want to build a team from social media, you need to follow the process and the principles of working on social media which I call a social media sales funnel. It's a 5-step process that will empower you to convert strangers into your teammates. You need to learn and do things as per this process and slowly start integrating social media and online business-building tools into your total sales process. This process has been explained in Illustration 9.

Step #1. Building your brand

The first step is to register your presence on social media. Open your accounts and start posting. Creating value-adding content and posting it as per the best strategies is the first step in the funnel and it helps establish your brand. After a few months of consistent posting, people will start taking you seriously and associate your brand values with your name. What you post consistently builds your brand. Everything you need to do for building your brand on social media has been covered extensively in this book.

Illustration 9

Source – *Ultimate Network Marketing Mastery*, a 91-day online course by Deepak Bajaj

Step #2. Lead generation

After posting, we want people to engage with our posts. We need likes and comments on our posts, but please realize the critical difference – we are not interested in *how* many likes, but we want to track *who* is liking and commenting on our posts. This is where the real work begins. People who are liking and commenting are giving you a clear signal that they are interested in you and your work. But what do you do when someone makes eye contact with you or extends his or her hand for a handshake? You respond instantly. Would you not do the same on social media? Likes on a post are similar to extending a hand for a handshake. Your posts have made people make the first move by liking your posts. So just as you respond instantly to a handshake, you must respond immediately to a like or comment. Make it a policy to message everyone who has liked your post on the very same day.

> *"Getting the Like is easy. It's a light action.*
> *Anything else requires trust."*
> — Jon Loomer

Step #3. Starting a relationship

When you message someone who has liked or commented on your post, you initiate the process of starting a relationship. They have written their comment right below your posts. Those comments are public. You can reply to the comments right there and start the conversation, but the smartest thing to do is to move this conversation from the public space to a private space. How do you do that? Send them a private message on Facebook Messenger or DM them on Instagram. Send a private message to everyone who likes your posts on the same day. Does it sound like too much work? Yes, it is too much work, but if you don't do this then all the effort of creating and posting awesome content has totally gone to waste. Never forget the golden rule:

Posting + Conversation = Results

Step #4. Strengthening your relationship

For all those conversations that are moving forward in a positive direction on Facebook Messenger or in Instagram DMs, exchange phone numbers and move those conversations to WhatsApp or phone calls. Moving from step 1 to step 4 will take different time for different people. For many people, it may stop at step 2 and for some others, it may reach up to step 3 or 4. Your job is to keep moving conversations forward in this social media sales funnel. Don't force anything. Every person is unique and every relationship is different. Just go with the flow. The top 1% of income earners travel this journey smoothly with posture and without being desperate. If you continue creating and posting good-quality content consistently, you will never be short of prospects; then keep moving all new prospects along this sales funnel.

> *"Content builds relationships. Relationships are built on trust. Trust drives revenue."*
>
> — ANDREW DAVIS

Step #5. Approaching them for business

Whenever you feel that the time is right, approach them to share your business opportunity or products using any of the methods you deem suitable for this person.

Please note and understand that inviting people for a business opportunity happens at step 5, not at step 1. Every day I receive this one question from hundreds of people on Instagram, Facebook and YouTube: how do you invite strangers to do business with you on social media? I am sure you would have got your answer in this chapter. You never invite people for your business opportunity presentation on social media. The role of social media is only for expanding your list and prospecting. You identify people on social media, start conversations and gradually move the conversation from public spaces to private messaging, WhatsApp and phone calls. After that, the normal sales process that we have been following for our regular prospects will be followed. An invitation does not happen on social media, an invitation happens on a phone call, video call or face-to-face meeting.

The biggest disaster people make on social media is to share their meeting invitation and Zoom meeting links on their social media page. On top of that, they expect people to click on those links and actually turn up for the meetings. I advise you not to skip the steps. It has never given anyone any results and it will never give you any either. I have seen thousands of direct sellers who keep looking for shortcuts and waste years without any success. Why not follow the process and build such a system that you will never be short of prospects? This funnel that I have explained here is a shortcut anyway; please don't look for an even shorter route.

> *"Success on social media doesn't depend on the number of followers; it's about how many people you can connect with."*
> — DEEPAK BAJAJ

As you master the social media sales funnel, you must learn two more things to build and manage your business online:

1. Online tools

Tools are amazing and they can accelerate the business-building process. The best thing about tools is that they work even when you are not working. Tools are easily duplicable and multiply your working hours. Regular use of tools is the only way to build a business that runs on autopilot and continues to give you passive income generation after generation.

What are tools? Anything that your prospects may ask or anything that you think can help you move faster with prospecting and sales closing process can be termed as tools. Books, videos, audios, catalogues, presentations, brochures, ebooks etc. are all different forms of tools. Don't wait for people to ask you something; start building your toolkit in advance. Teach your teammates to also use tools aggressively.

2. Online meetings and training

Social media has dissolved boundaries and made the whole world accessible to you through your phone. You don't know where your next prospect will be located. So master the techniques and software for conducting online meetings and training.

In conclusion, there are 3 components of building a business online that you need to master:

1. Social media sales funnel
2. Online tools
3. Online meetings and training

Mastering this is a deeper subject. You can do it on your own or seek help from one of my most popular online training programs that is 3 weeks long, called *Social Media and Online Business Mastery*. This online course comes with free access to my private mentorship group where you can collaborate and work with thousands of other direct sellers from across the globe and also get 24/7 lifetime support.

In the last couple of years, a new hybrid-working model has evolved in direct selling industry that I call the SOTO working model. This SOTO working model has 4 key components that are essential now for success in the direct selling business. Earlier, these 4 components were optional but from 2020 onwards, especially after the COVID-19 pandemic, using all these 4 components has become compulsory for building a direct selling business. These 4 components have been displayed in Illustration 10.

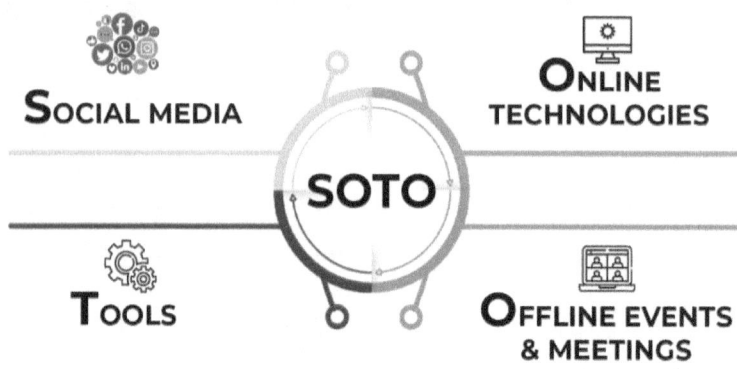

Illustration 10

A lot of people have asked me this question: "Will online business and social media replace offline meetings and events?" The answer is "no". As you start building your business with social media, the share of your online business in your total business will gradually start increasing. You will continue using your existing system and start integrating the social media sales funnel wherever you can.

Now you have both online and offline business-building models and tools. You have greater flexibility and more options to build and expand your business.

- Use social media and online technologies for list expansion, prospecting, team retention, presentations, training, building your brand, exploring new markets, highlighting your achievements etc.

- Use offline events and meetings to build relationships, sales closing, building faith, product expansion, take off of new associates etc.

New avenues and possibilities have opened up for direct sellers who are committed to grow and expand their business. Just like with every tool and technology, it's entirely up to your creativity as to how you want to apply them in your business.

> *"If your business is not on the Internet, then your business will be out of business."*
> — BILL GATES

Many of my online course participants have reported a new shift in their work habits that has multiplied their income up to five times for the same time and effort. Let me illustrate how they have achieved this. One of the key activities for any direct seller is face-to-face or one-to-one business opportunity presentation. Every direct seller has to travel for such meetings. The whole business presentation may take 60-90 minutes and travel takes another 1-2 hours. So on average, it takes 2-3 hours per business presentation. Some of the meetings may also get cancelled. If you consider an average conversion rate of 20%, the time spent on getting one new sale is 12-15 hours. This equals 1-2 weeks of the time any part-time direct seller devotes to his or her business.

After mastering the various components of the SOTO model, smart direct sellers have now started doing a lot of their work using online tools and technologies. All activities like preparing the prospect for the business opportunity, prospecting, qualifying them for business, sharing basic details, delivering business or product presentations etc. now take place online. It cuts out the travel time and saves you from giving presentations to people who are not really serious about building the business.

After all the basic information has been shared and one or two online meetings have already taken place, now these new-age smart direct sellers are doing face-to-face meetings only once a week for all those prospects who have studied all the basic material and are interested in knowing more. Many direct sellers have stopped doing face-to-face meetings for business opportunity presentations and clarifying all basic doubts. Face-to-face meetings are done only for CRS – Confidence building, Reassurance and Sales closing. This single shift has raised their confidence and income by many times. Along with an increase in income, imagine what they could do with all the free time that was wasted in travel every single day.

Master all components of the SOTO model and make the best of everything to exponentially grow your business. Please don't stop experimenting and adapting as things change. Don't wait for things to change; become an agent of change and adapt faster than everybody else to lead a new revolution of online direct selling.

> *"Random social media tactics lead to random results. You need a strategy."*
>
> — STEPHANIE SAMMONS

REMEMBER AND SHARE

- If you want to build a team from social media, you need to follow the complete process and the principles of working on social media.
- Posting regularly on social media is only 20% of the total work that you need to do if you want to recruit people online. You cannot recruit people if you don't do the other 80% of work too.
- While tracking likes and comments on your social media posts, don't worry about how many likes you get, but track who is liking and commenting on your posts.
- Approach people and invite them for the business opportunity presentation only when you think that the time is right for them to share the presentation. Continue prospecting until that time.
- You cannot recruit a single person from social media if you don't complement it with these two things: online tools and online meetings.
- The SOTO hybrid working model is the future of direct selling.

KEY ACTIONS TO TAKE

- Identify which area of the social media sales funnel you have been missing and make an action plan for following it completely.
- Build your toolkit with online tools that will help you in prospecting, sales closing and business multiplication.
- Identify which areas from the SOTO model you will integrate into your daily working.

CHAPTER 14

15 Principles and Strategies for Online Business Multiplication

"It's much easier to double your business by doubling your conversion rate than by doubling your traffic."

— Jeff Eisenberg

ALL THE WORK THAT I have done in the last two decades including my books, live training, videos, social media content and online courses have been centered around one key theme – change and transformation. I believe if any course or training is not able to deliver results and bring about the desired transformation, it is a failure. The same goes for this book. My aim for creating this book is simple – you should not waste any time on social media. You must get maximum results for the time that you invest on social media. So if you implement everything we have covered so far, you are set to get massive results from your social media efforts. To seal it further, I want to share with you 15 key principles and strategies that will empower you to multiply your results manifold.

"Marketers need to build digital relationships and reputation before closing a sale."

— Chris Brogan

Business Multiplier #1
Actively participate in similar interest groups

There are so many groups available on Facebook, and well-managed groups have a thriving community of like-minded people who are engaged in excellent conversations. If you can identify the right groups and participate in ongoing conversations, you have great opportunities to connect with potential prospects.

I have also observed that more than 80% of the members in any group are silent. They never comment or post anything. Out of the remaining 20%, there are only 1-2% that actively contribute to the group; the rest only like posts or reply with some emojis.

Just like everywhere else in life, there is also enough space in Facebook groups to be among the top 1% of active members. I highly recommend you follow this one rule that I personally follow – either be among the top 1% of active members or exit the group. Remember: no conversations, no business. On top of that, don't just engage in conversations but also promote the group. Be an evangelist or self-appointed spokesperson of the group – promote it, comment, share, post and engage in conversations. Be seen in the group. These groups can be your goldmines. Use them smartly.

Another piece of expert advice regarding Facebook groups – please make sure you choose the right groups and never forget that there are endless groups available, so exit quickly if the conversations, themes, members' profiles etc. are not matching what you are looking for.

Business Multiplier #2
Ask the right questions

As you master the art of meaningful conversations, you should also develop the acumen to ask the right questions. Right from contacting strangers to prospecting and follow-through, your real job is to keep asking smart questions in a conversational style and ultimately lead them to where you want them to go. Asking the right questions is your edge. Whether it's an online conversation or offline, the right questions help you identify how much to reveal at what stage and how fast or slow to proceed with them. The right questions also help you maintain your posture.

Business Multiplier #3
Keep the exit option open

Always give an exit option when prospecting. Don't make every conversation feel like a life-or-death matter. Let it be open; have fun and go with the flow. Your prospects will respect you and feel good about you. That's how your friendship has a chance to continue; otherwise, one meeting could be the end of all the efforts that you have put in. Have the faith that you are on a mission to help people live better lives and a lot of the right people will start with you. Pushing too hard in the early stages of the conversation never yields the desired results.

Business Multiplier #4
Prospecting pool

On 28 June 2007, I started my network marketing business part-time along with my job. After 3 months, on 30 September 2007, I resigned my job to take up network marketing full-time. I worked non-stop right from the first day, made many mistakes, lost many teams, faced a lot of rejection and ridicule and experimented with so many different working styles, but one and a half years after starting my business, I was able to establish a system that started giving me passive income. From January 2009 onwards, I started getting passive income from my network marketing business. But I continued my personal sponsoring and recruited 2-4 new associates to my team every single week. I continued building my width and depth. I was busy with events every single day but my personal sponsoring continued effortlessly. Do you want to know the secret?

After 18 months of non-stop working in the field, I had created a bank of more than 5,000 people who I was in touch with. Every week, I used to choose 8-10 people from this bank of prospects who were ready for my business opportunity presentation. After making mistakes with hundreds of people, I truly understood that sharing business opportunity presentations without adequate prospecting was a total waste of time. I used to continue my prospecting until people were excited about building a business with me.

I used to share my opportunity with 8-10 such qualified prospects every week and closed 2-4 new personal sales in that time. Not only did I sponsor 2-4 new people every week, but also every sale in those days meant a good amount of shopping, and not just some basic purchase of 1,000-2,000 rupees. I had gradually created my own system of closing sales before showing the presentation.

I meet so many direct sellers that are still struggling with prospects who don't pick up their calls after seeing the business presentation, and such direct sellers keep blaming the business or negativity in the market for not getting results. Please remember it's not a failure of the business; it's a failure of the people who are not doing the business in the right way. Actually, such direct sellers are bypassing an important activity of the direct selling sales process that I call the prospecting pool.

I always say that nobody can ever build a big business with posture and happiness without an ever-growing prospecting pool. If you don't know about it, a prospecting pool is a large group of people with whom you are in different stages of conversation. Learn how to create your prospecting pool and you will never be short of prospects to speak to.

When I first introduced this concept in my 91-day online program, *Ultimate Network Marketing Mastery*, people were skeptical. Most of the network marketers had never heard of a prospecting pool, closing sales before the presentation etc. On top of that, people thought that network marketing could be learned in 2-3 hours, so why did they need 91 days for the same? But today, if I ask my course participants what their most valuable learning from the course was, irrespective of the country, product, company or income model they are working with, most of the participants admit that mastering the total process of building their never-ending prospecting pool was their #1 learning from the *Ultimate Network Marketing Mastery* course. While 99% of direct sellers keep chasing a limited number of prospects for months, imagine your life and growth if you had a big pool of prospects from which you choose whom you would share your business opportunity with. It can totally change your game. So start building your prospecting pool today.

> *"Marketing takes a day to learn.*
> *Unfortunately it takes a lifetime to master."*
> — Phil Kotler

Business Multiplier #5
Never lose your posture

Posture is the real ornament of a direct seller. Posture is your total belief in what you have and how you present yourself to others, regardless of what others think or any external approval. This means when a friend or family member tells you that your business is a scam or pyramid scheme, you proceed without feeling embarrassed or getting defensive.

That's where posture comes in – not in fighting with everyone, everywhere, but in knowing that you have the best to offer. You have posture when you believe you are in the right business and you trust that you are building the business with the right set of values and principles.

Business Multiplier #6
Use the power of stories

The biggest mistake people make in sales closing, especially smart people with good communication skills, is that they talk endlessly and continue showing off their knowledge. But the top leaders in network marketing tell stories. When you talk, you tend to give statistics, examples, motivation or information. Most of the statistics that you share are true, but all these are logical reasons to start the business. Stories appeal to the emotional aspect of decision-making. Based on my two decades of experience working with and training people, I can tell you that people move when their emotions are moved.

People take the decision to start doing business with us through emotions; they use logic just to validate their decision. Stories connect with their heart and spur them to action. Most of the people who you will approach for network marketing would have already heard about it or may have even tried their hands at it with one or more network marketing companies. Most of the time, they will have already heard information or statistics similar to what you are giving them from someone in the past. What make your business presentation unique are you and your stories.

Master the art of storytelling. Let your stories do the talking. Tell your story or stories from your uplines or teammates at every meeting while handling any objections. Please remember that storytelling is not about showing off your achievements; rather, it's about making them connect deeply with you. What is most important when you tell your story is your background before you started the business and what made you start the business. Share your struggles and weaknesses. If you want to know how to tell your stories in the most impactful manner, please refer to my 7-step formula for storytelling in my book *Be a Network Marketing Millionaire*.

When you are willing to be vulnerable and truthful with the other person, they will be truthful with you and it will start a real conversation. You can build a relationship faster when you share your struggles, not when you pretend to be cool and invincible. Another advantage of telling stories is that it makes you seem real and does not make you look like a salesperson. As you become one among them, it opens the door. Answer every objection with a story. The best network marketers are the best storytellers.

Business Multiplier #7
Emotionally detach yourself from the outcome

Be committed to your goals. Aim for the best results. But at the same time, don't take rejections and ridicule to heart. Some people will say no. You also say no at so many different places every single day. Don't take it personally. It's no to the business proposal and not to you. No simply means that the time is not right for them right now. Move them to your quarterly follow-through list, maintain communication with them and check in after 3-6 months. Things change. I started my business after 13 months of initial discussion with my upline. I have recruited hundreds of people more than 6 months after our first conversation. I have seen hundreds of cases where people started the business 3-5 years after seeing the presentation.

> *"All the NOs you are getting today are building your next year's sales."*
>
> — Deepak Bajaj

Remember the famous SWSWSWSW Rule – Some Will, Some Won't. So What? Someone is Waiting.

Business Multiplier #8
Always work like a consultant and a well-wisher

Sales closing is not pushing or forcing people, it's guiding them to do what is right for them. Give them the confidence that it's not you vs. them, it's you and them together as a team to fulfill both of your dreams faster. Make it easier for them to take the decision by saying lines like "Let's work together", "Try it out", "You and me", "Let's collaborate", "Give it a shot", "What's there to lose" etc. Always help them choose products or services that are most appropriate for them and not what will give you higher profits or business volume.

> *"Sales closing is not the end of the process in direct selling, it's the beginning."*
>
> — Deepak Bajaj

Business Multiplier #9
Honor your teammates with recognition posts

As you establish your income and leadership in network marketing, start using recognition posts to multiply your business. Recognition posts work like magic and give you multiple benefits. They are the ones where you highlight some of your teammates' achievements on your page. But when you are posting these, never include the phrase 'network marketing' in your post or description. Show the photo, talk about benefits or results but never give details about the company, product or business opportunity. Don't write phrases like "Joined with me", "Diamond", "Bronze director", "Network marketing rocks", "Income statements" etc.

Business Multiplier #10
Build your community

Social media is an excellent platform to build your community. A community is built with conversations. People like and comment on your posts, photos and videos and you also do the same, and it feels like a family; a community that cares. When you bring your entire team together on social media, you will be able to communicate to every one of them irrespective of where they are in your line of sponsorship. Social media works round the clock irrespective of geographical boundaries and makes your people feel closer to you.

> *"The secret to getting results from your social networking is to act like a member, not a marketer."*
> — MARI SMITH

Business Multiplier #11
Use social media to demonstrate the right practices and quickly introduce new tools

As your business starts growing in different locations, you can use social media to instantly demonstrate the right practices to your teammates irrespective of their location and placement. Whatever you want your team to follow, just show them photos or videos of you doing those activities on your social media page. When they see you doing those activities consistently, they will start doing the same without waiting for you to tell them to do it. There's a famous saying in network marketing that people don't do what you tell them to do, people do what you do. As your teammates start seeing your actions, they will immediately start copying the same.

Social media can accelerate the speed of your communication across your entire team. If you found a new testimony or a new document that could help your teammates, just share it on your social media profile and it will instantly reach your teammates. Post your new video on YouTube and it will be accessible to the world instantly. You can share its link on Facebook and other platforms to make it accessible to them as well.

Business Multiplier #12
Take absolute ownership of your business

> *"You can come into this business by chance but you cannot become a millionaire by chance."*
> — DEEPAK BAJAJ

Since this business starts with almost zero investment and there is no accountability, 99% of the people don't take ownership of the business and get out of the business without even realizing what it could have done for them. Never think about what have you invested to start the business; rather, think about what this business could give you if you build it seriously in the right way.

Almost everybody starts this business with a part-time attitude, but most of the people use this part-time tag as an excuse for their non-performance. Please remember it's not about part-time or full-time; it's about doing the right activities at the right time with the right system. Businesses are never part-time or full-time; it's your attitude. I write books, I make videos and posts for social media, I do training and consulting, I create new tools for helping people succeed faster and a lot more. Which activity is full-time and which one is part-time? Throw away all excuses and take complete ownership of your business. Your business starts with you. Work with an attitude of *"I will either find a way or create a way."*

Business Multiplier #13
Smart day management

I have always said this in all my live talks and training events: network marketing is less about selling and more about time management. I have observed that people are excellent at setting their life goals and 10-year goals, but they are miserable when it comes to managing their days. One of the key skills you need to master for massive success in this business and in life is to manage your day smartly, especially if you are a part-timer; you must become super efficient with your time.

Make this business the center of your life; everything else should be managed around this. Learn to say "no" to some invitations. Guard your time. Use evening hours and weekends judiciously for doing core business activities. Do group meetings instead of one-to-one meetings wherever you can. Use breaks smartly to finish business tasks.

Business Multiplier #14
Be open to learn from all possible sources

Every direct seller knows that the more you learn, the more you earn. Direct selling companies and teams are known for massive training but the tragedy is that most of the training is repetitive and outdated. Most of the training programs in network marketing companies are nothing more than some religious talks (*satsangs*) or motivational seminars where most of the people just tell stories in the name of training. Most of the training begins and ends with this one line: "*If I can do it, then you can also do it.*" This is fine, and it can feel good for a short time. But what will help your team survive and thrive is complete training on skills, mindset, tools and techniques. Network marketing training urgently needs to shift from motivation and stories to real skills and strategies.

We are living in an information economy. The rise of social media, growing internet penetration, surge of new technologies and growing transparency have made the best training accessible to everyone. You just need to decide what skills, tools and techniques you need for your success and find the best mentors and programs for the same. The fastest-growing network marketers have already started taking professional training and coaching from industry experts along with regular training from their uplines and company. Just one word of caution – when you decide to choose your coach and trainer, choose someone who is genuine, who has actually done what he or she is teaching and who has an incredible track record.

> *"Getting the like is easy. It's a light action. Anything else requires trust."*
> — JON LOOMER

Business Multiplier #15
Master the entire process and do not look for shortcuts

Every day, people ask me so many questions on social media, like "How can I invite people?", "How do I close the maximum number of sales?", "How do I retain people?", "How can I become a great leader?" etc. These are not questions to be answered in the chat in one word or one line. People want to become overnight millionaires in network marketing but are not interested in learning the principles and processes for succeeding in this business. This business is just like any other business. It offers huge opportunities and possibilities, but only for those who are committed to learn and practice the rules of this business.

Network marketing is not a get-rich-quick scheme or lottery. It's not a game of luck or chance. It's a proven business that has been successfully helping people since the 1940s in almost 200 countries across the globe. This business has been consistently growing and has generated a revenue of Rs. 13.5 lakh crores in 2019 as per the WFDSA annual report for 2020. I think this business deserves much more seriousness and commitment than most people generally give it.

This is my 15th year of being closely associated with this business and I have trained more than 11 lakh direct sellers. I can tell you with absolute certainty that this business is a shortcut to help you fulfill your dreams, but there are no shortcuts to success in this business. Stay away from people, leaders, trainers and programs that are trying to sell you something in the name of quick returns or shortcuts. Be committed to building a big business and mastering the entire process for a successful long-term career in network marketing. Rise every day and be a source of strength and inspiration for fellow direct sellers. Together, let's bring some more pride and glory to this incredible profession.

> *"Never start a business just to make money.
> Start a business to make a difference."*
> — MARIE FORLEO

REMEMBER AND SHARE

- One of the key abilities you need to develop is the art of asking the right questions to your prospects or teammates, online and offline.
- Start building your prospecting pool today. Once you have a big enough and ever-growing prospecting pool, you will never be short of prospects to speak to.
- Build your business with posture and work like a consultant or well-wisher for your prospects.
- Build your community and uplift everyone in your team with the right practices and tools.
- It's your business. It starts with you. Take complete ownership of your business.
- Continue learning from multiple sources, never look for shortcuts and master the entire business-building process.

KEY ACTIONS TO TAKE

- Identify 5 key strategies from this chapter that you will start implementing immediately in your business.
- Share these 5 learnings with your team.

CHAPTER 15

Use Social Media, but Don't Let It Use You – 5 Traps To Avoid

> *"Social media is addictive precisely because it gives us something, which the real world lacks: it gives us immediacy, direction and value as an individual."*
>
> — DAVID AMERLAND

So far in this book, I have talked endlessly about the benefits and possibilities of social media. Undeniably, social media is an incredible tool and it can definitely take your personal brand and business to unprecedented heights of success. But just like with any other tool, there are some areas of concern that may stop you from reaping the full benefit of this amazing resource. I want to quickly highlight some of those areas of concern in this chapter so that you can effectively use social media and not let it use you.

#1. Don't trust everything you see

Social media and the internet have made all information easily accessible at your fingertips, but the only challenge is that everything you see on social media and internet is not true. Actually, there is no check on what is being written and who is writing it. Every third person claims himself or herself to be an expert or guru. A big chunk of what you see on the internet and social media has been set up there with paid advertisements and digital marketing. The onus of checking the authenticity of the information and using it properly has been left entirely to the user.

That's why I highly recommend that one of the key skills to develop right now is the maturity and intelligence to decide whom to listen to and what to follow. So take information only from reliable sources and carefully choose whom to follow. Anyway, you don't need too much information or too many coaches to be successful. Identify a few reliable sources and industry leaders and focus on implementing what you learn from them.

#2. Guard your time

Another thing you need to be careful about when you are on social media is to be aware of how much time you are spending on social media. You have to guard your time on social media. There is an entry door for social media, but no exit door. Don't stay for 2 hours if you had only come for 5 minutes. Spending more time on social media has no relation to your success.

#3. Never compare yourself with anyone

Don't beat yourself up by looking at what others have been posting. Nobody posts his or her failures or struggles on social media. I don't want to make generic comments or statements about what is good or bad, but I know that one thing is for sure: you are unique and you have a unique journey. You never know anybody else's journey – when they started, what their objective is, why they are doing what they are doing etc. Everyone is unique and everyone is on his or her own journey. Don't judge others and at the same time, never compare yourself with others. Always remember your own mission and continue moving forward in the direction of your goal.

> *"The biggest insult you can give to yourself and to your creator is to compare yourself with others."*
> — Deepak Bajaj

#4. Social media is a part of life and not the whole of it

Never, ever forget the distinction that social media is one small part of your life and not the whole of it. It is tragic to see so many people who are so lost in social media that they just forget everyone around them and fail to establish a genuine human connection.

You will see so many couples in restaurants who have taken time out for the dinner but instead of being with each other, they are busy with their mobile phones. Instead of enjoying the meal, they are busy posting pictures and then waiting for likes and comments on their photo. You will see parents who are watching their kids dance but instead of watching them dance, they are busy making a video to post on social media. People go to lovely places but instead of enjoying the beauty of those places, they are more concerned about taking pictures and posting them. After posting photos and videos, counting the likes and comments becomes the next big worry.

Please note that I am not against posting photos or videos on social media, but I am against sacrificing your valuable time with the dearest people in your life for those who may not even care for your posts. I want you to remember that posting everything is not mandatory. You can live life without posting on social media. Don't be under this pressure that you need to post everything. Strike a balance. Enjoy every moment. Capture memories in your phone and post them if you like it. Give more priority to real life than just the reel life. The person sitting in front of you is definitely more important than someone who will watch your photos or videos on social media.

> *"One of the most important things about social media is knowing when to put the phone down and experience your life."*
>
> — TAYLOR SWIFT

#5. Never judge yourself and your work with the number of likes or comments you get

I want to remind you one more time that your uniqueness is your greatest power. Your voice, your message and your work are important. You never know who needs what you have. Please don't judge yourself and the quality of your work with the number of likes or comments you get. That is the wrong yardstick with which to evaluate yourself. I have seen lot of genuine people who stopped sharing their message just because they did not get a large audience.

> *"The size of your audience is a reflection of many factors that are not in your control, but the quality of work that you produce is something that is totally in your control. So focus on what you can control."*
>
> — DEEPAK BAJAJ

Social media is not a tool but a revolution. It's a proof of human evolution. As we humans evolve together, social media will also evolve. Continue growing with the same and creatively find more and more applications of this incredible medium to uplift your game and to live a life of impact and contribution.

REMEMBER AND SHARE

- Social media is an incredible tool; use it but never let it use you.
- Social media is free; your time is not. Develop the maturity and intelligence to decide whom to listen to and what to follow.
- Never compare yourself and your work with anybody else.
- People's likes or comments don't define you.
- Social media is one part of your life and not the whole of it.

KEY ACTIONS TO TAKE

- Introspect and check if you have been affected by any of the 5 traps that we have discussed in this chapter.

The Next Steps

"I can do things you cannot, you can do things I cannot; together we can do great things."

— MOTHER TERESA

CONGRATULATIONS ON COMPLETING THIS book. It clearly shows your willingness to learn and grow. I appreciate your commitment. But I believe each one of us has infinite potential to learn more and grow more. This book has given you a very good foundation, but I don't want you to stop here. I want you to fly higher and higher and hence, I have a few quick recommendations for you as you continue your journey from becoming good to great.

#1. Take action – Knowledge is not power; knowledge becomes power when it is applied. Take action and implement what you have learned. Experiment with different concepts and uplift your game on social media. As you implement them, if you have any queries or challenges, get in touch with me and my team on any of our social media accounts or email us. It will be our pleasure to serve you again.

#2. Sharing is caring – If you got some ideas or value from this book, please share them whole-heartedly with as many people as you can – your family, friends, teammates, and anyone you care about. You can help a countless number of people simply by sharing about this book on WhatsApp, Instagram, Facebook, Telegram, YouTube and whichever other platforms you can. I thank you in advance for the same.

#3. Get on board our social media mastery program – If you want to explore many more ways to build your brand and start using social media for expanding your life and business, I highly recommend our online program, *Social Media and Online Business Mastery*. It's a one-of-a-kind program with 23 comprehensive lessons covering the A to Z of everything you need to build your brand and grow your business online with social media. Every day, we cover one different topic along with dedicated tasks and assignments delivered using a unique NLP-based methodology to deliver amazing results and transformation. You can join me on this course right away, on the click of a button at www.deepakbajaj.biz.

#4. Review and feedback – I would really appreciate it if you could share your valuable feedback on this book or any of my other work that you have come across. Please share your reviews for this book on Amazon and Flipkart. Your suggestions on anything that you want me to add or change in this book or any other of our books, videos etc. are heartily welcomed.

#5. Join our community – We have a large global community of like-minded individuals on different social media platforms where I share invaluable cutting-edge information and tools regularly. It's absolutely free and you can learn a lot from this global community. Join us right now for free through our Instagram, Facebook and other main social media accounts.

> "A real decision is measured by the fact that you have taken a new action. If there is no action, you haven't truly decided."
>
> — TONY ROBBINS

We have one of the largest range of tools, online courses and training programs for life and business excellence, especially for network marketers, including free video training, free ebooks, live workshops, books, high-performance coaching and more. My team and I would be happy to serve you and help you on your journey to success.

I am always with you on every step of your journey to your dream life.

Your friend, partner and well-wisher,
Deepak Bajaj

Feedback/queries – support@deepakbajaj.biz
www.deepakbajaj.biz

Deepak Bajaj's High-Performance Solutions for Life and Business Excellence

*Every next level of success demands
a different version of you.*

FOR ALMOST TWO DECADES, I have been passionately obsessed with creating tools and training for empowering people to **accomplish their dreams easier and faster**. In fact, inspiring and empowering people is my life's mission and that of my organization. My books, talks, videos, online courses, workshops and everything else that I do are centered on this mission. I strongly believe that each one of us has the seeds of greatness inside us and we all can do amazing achievements with the right inspiration, mentoring, training and guidance. My team and I want to contribute in your journey to success, happiness and abundance through our research-based, practical, proven and constantly evolving tools and solutions.

All my tools and training have been designed with one clear goal – it should bring **instant change and lasting transformation**. Any change and the next level of transformation are possible only when you upgrade your knowledge, skills, mindset, toolset and emotional quotient simultaneously. What you need is a holistic mindset and skills-based training, not just motivation. Motivation is temporary; skills and transformation are permanent. Team Deepak Bajaj has got one of the biggest range of resources available for success in direct selling and any other area in life. You can get all the updated details on our website (www.deepakbajaj.biz) and our social media accounts. Here is a glimpse of our major tools and solutions:

> *"There is no secret to success;
> there is always a system to success."*
> — DEEPAK BAJAJ

#1. Free Video Training – Deepak's YouTube channel is considered one of the most trusted, transformative and biggest free training resources available online. It has got a large collection of life-changing videos full of knowledge, tools, ideas and techniques to take you to the next level. You can find videos on direct selling or network marketing, relationships, team-building, success, goals, success, social media mastery, leadership, time management, life management, public speaking, communication and a lot of other subjects over at www.youtube.com/deepakbajaj. As of writing of this book, 6,50,000 plus people from 100-plus countries are learning and growing every day with this channel.

#2. Online Courses – You can master the best international knowledge, tools, skills and ideas right from the comfort of your home with our online courses. These courses have been designed and delivered with a unique NLP-based methodology and activity-based learning that brings you the desired results from every course. You can access them anywhere, anytime on our website and mobile apps.

#3. Books – What you are holding in your hand is the third book by Deepak Bajaj. Deepak's other two books, *Achieve More, Succeed Faster* and *Be a Network Marketing Millionaire*, have been among the most-read and most-followed books in the direct selling industry. These are essential guidebooks that have already provided excellent results to lakhs of direct sellers across the globe, irrespective of their company, products or income plan. You can order them online or get them from any bookstore near you. Deepak has written some excellent ebooks as well that you can download from our website (www.deepakbajaj.biz) totally free of cost.

#4. Live Workshops – Deepak's live workshops are famous for their incredible energy and real transformation that begins right during the workshop. As of writing of this book, more than 11 lakh people have already attended these workshops and training events. These workshops are always sold out due to their unique methodology, result-delivering activities, best international course material, transformative tools and real-life techniques.

#5. High-Performance Coaching – For those who want to achieve nothing but the best and at jet speeds, there is a high-performance coaching program where Deepak will personally work with you with customized solutions to take you or your organization to the next level of excellence with whatever you choose – health, happiness, profitability, business multiplication, emotional challenges etc.

#6. Keynote Speeches – Deepak has been regularly invited by corporates, universities, government organizations and different independent bodies to deliver his unique, electrifying and transformative speeches that not only motivate the audience but also produce the desired results. These speeches are generally from 30 minutes to 2 hours long and are customized as per the needs of the organizers. Deepak works with a unique 6-component formula to deliver transformation with every speech.

#7. Customized Training – Deepak and his team conduct customized training on a variety of subjects for corporates, universities, government organizations, direct selling companies and direct selling teams. Deepak's corporate experience, international NLP certification and 18 years of training experience with more than 11 lakh people brings instant change and lasting transformation with every training he conducts. Deepak is the number one choice for training for all major network marketing companies.

#8. Corporate Consultations – Deepak has been consulting for companies to help them achieve their goals faster through customized consultations that include brand building, corporate identity, social media, sales, organizational policies, business multiplication and many more core areas.

Get all the necessary information at:
www.deepakbajaj.biz.

"The end of one journey is the beginning of another."
— DEEPAK BAJAJ

Looking forward to meeting you again soon.

Acknowledgements

My sincere gratitude to each and every one of my readers, YouTube subscribers, social media followers, workshop participants, coaching clients, teammates and all of you who have touched my life with your presence and wisdom. Every interaction with you has deeply impacted me and made me the person I am today. You have been bestowing me with ever-growing love, support and prayers. What you all have done for me has been invaluable and I can never thank you enough for that. This book is all yours. Thanks a lot.

Behind everything I do, I have an incredible 24/7 support system – my family. I am lucky to have found all of these in my family – my best friends, companions, partners, advisors, cheerleaders and my biggest supporters. I am nothing without all the love, care, support, affection and inspiration you all give me. Thank you Papa, Mamma, Tanima, Gaurav, Divya, Devanshi, Cheeraayu, Prashansa, Nirbhay and Saksham.

My special gratitude to my brother and partner Gaurav Bajaj. He is the backbone behind all our achievements. I believe he is the best direct selling leader on Earth.

www.ingramcontent.com/pod-product-compliance
Lightning Source LLC
Chambersburg PA
CBHW031622210526
45464CB00004B/1708